CULTURAL CONTACT BETWEEN INDIA & CENTRAL ASIA

VEN RAVI MEDHANKAR
INTERNATIONAL PRESIDENT
WORLD BUDDHIST MISSION Japan

NOTION PRESS

Year 2023

NOTION PRESS

India. Singapore. Malaysia.

ISBN -979-8889860549

Year of Publication - 2023

Dedicated to my parents

PREMLATA & M.N. SINGH
(FORMER DUPTY DIRECTOR ADULT EDUCATION GOVT. OF BIHAR)

Contents

FORWARD

Honoured by the Hon'ble Governor of
Bihar
DR. MAHESH KUMAR SHARAN
M.A. (A.I.&A.S.), M.A. (Hist.), Ph.D.,
D.Litt., D.R.S.
Former University Professor and Head
P.G. Department of Ancient Indian &
Asian Studies,
GAYA COLLEGE, GAYA
(Magadh University, Bodhgaya), Bihar
Former GUEST FELLOW
MAHA CHULALONGKORN BUDDHIST UNIVERSITY,
BANGKOK (THAILAND)

For Correspondence
APARAJITA
26 R, Bank Colony,
Padari Bazar, Piparaich Road,
Gorakhpur, (U.P.), 273014 mob. -
6393771493, 9452778554
Email id-maheshsharan653@gmail.com

Dr. Medhankar Ravi's book is a welcome edition. He has worked with commendable patience and devotion and has published this book that would help in understanding Lord Buddha's teachings and human suffering.

May the present publication prove to be an important milestone in extending world peace since the teachings of Lord are for the benefit of entire humankind. Also, it will go a long way in removing the feeling of hatred and tension and jealousy among the people. The universe is one, the humanity is one and the key to open it is also one. Here lies the greatness of Buddhism with the message of peace, amity, and universalism.

Sab be sattasukhihontu

Sarvebhavantusukhinah

Let all biengs be happy

I have great pleasure in congratulating Dr. Medhankar, one of my brilliant students of the Magadh University Bodhgaya - the sacred place of the Buddhist World who himself converted to Buddhism for the propagation of the message of the Lord.

I bless, Dr. Medhankar for his long life so that He may bring out some more sacred and valuable books for orientation of a holy life of all human beings.

I have no doubt that his painstaking and scholarly work will receive due appreciation from the learned scholars on Buddhism of India and abroad.

(Mahesh Kumar Sharan)

ACKNOWLEDGEMENTS

I have no words to express my deep gratitude to Prof. Upendra Thakur under whom this work has been done and without his constant guidance and encouragement, this work would not have been possible.

I must express my profound gratitude and respect to my Professor Dr. Upendra Thakur, Head of the ANCIENT INDIAN AND ASIAN STUDIES department (POST-GRADUATE) MAGADH UNIVERSITY; BODHGAYA; my guide of "INDIAN ART IN CENTRAL ASIA", As DISSERTATION of Master of arts examination (session-1976- 78), under Whose holy feet I could learn ABC OF INDIAN HISTORY.

My thanks are due to Mrs. Chaya Bhattacharya, National Museum; New Delhi, our senior colleague who helped Me by explaining the findings from Central Asian ruins. My thanks are also due to the great scholar in This field for their remarkable contribution. as being bene- fitted in course of my present investigation.

I am grateful to my teacher Dr M. K. Sharan, Head of the A. I. & A. S. Department of Gaya COLLEGE, Gaya, and Dr. M. Aquique, lecturer in P. G. Department of A. I. & A. S. Magadh University, Bodhgaya, who helped me from very beginning.

I can not forget Dr. S. P. Gupta. Keeper, Central Asian antiquities department of the National Museum, New Delhi, who permitted me to have a look on the rare collection by sir A. Stein from deserted Central Asia, Dr. R. Gombrich, Professor of Indian Studies; OXFORD UNIVERSITY, for providing rare books on Central Asia. I am also indebted for the useful suggestions Provided by Dr. S. SAHAI, Dr R. C. Prasad, Dr. P. C. Roy, Dr. Birendra Singh and Dr. Y. K. Mishra of P. G. Department of A. I. & A. S. Magadh University, Bodhgaya.

My thankfulness knows no bounds to Mr. Ram Swaroop Singh, librarian, Superintending Archaeologist, Archaeological Survey of India, mid-eastern Circle, Patna in finding books and periodicals.

My thanks are also Tseu to Mr. Kamlesh Paswan research scholar at Nava Nalanda Mahavihara. Who made my dream true to publish this book, which was pending for a long time.

RAVI ANGSHUMAN (MEDHANKAR).

T.P.S. COLLEGE

INTRODUCTION

Cultural contact between India and Central Asia is a very important topic. Though few scholars of India as well as foreign countries have given a beam of light on different aspects of culture but no development has taken place in the field of India's cultural contribution to Central Asia after Bagchi and Chakravarthy. Being a student of department of Ancient Indian and Asian Studies I felt scarcity of books and periodicals, due to this it was difficult to carry on study in the field of Central Asia.

At the same time, we find a large number of materials available for the study of southeast- Asia but we have to means to study ser-India of Stein . Central Asia was the part of Asia where Indian colonies were established by Khotan, Niya, Kuchan, Turfan, Tibet, and inner Part of Mongolia. After review of the collection of art treasure gathered during explorations and excavations by eminent scholars of the world: - Russian (Beresovky and Kazaloff) Swedish (H.R. Tseu and R.P. Cobboid) British (MARC Aurel Stein .) Japanese (Count Kozui Otani, Horis, B. Akoi; Zuichi Tachibana) French (Prof. Paul Pelliot) German (Prof. A. Grunwedel, Dr.G. Huth; A. Von lacoq, Theodar Bartus). These materials tell us that the dominating people were Buddhist in nature while they were acquinted with other deities of India. People were mentally of Indian and Iranian origin. The earliest Chinese records and Niya documents along with Pali and Sanskrit texts recovered from different sites of Central Asia indicates that first hind kingdom in Central Asia was founded by the son of great Mauryan king Ashoka. Kuchian king Kumar Jiva also make it clear that Kucha was a seat of Hindu kingdom. Wall paintings, Buddhist sculpture, Terracotta, wooden crafts, Silk, linen, Banner, Leather pieces carved with ancient Indian literature were important among Central Asian findings.

These findings strengthen the view that the greater part of Central Asia was influenced with Indian cultural. People belonged to Central Asia were of mostly barbarous in nature, So, the civilization was far from them. with the rise of Buddhism Indian people came across the whole world. As Majumdar narrates, 'as in all ages and countries, the prospect of acquiring wealth first tempted the Indian traders and merchants to explore unknown territories beyond their own frontiers'.

From the accounts of Ptolemy, Geography of Marco Polo, Travel accounts of Fahien and Huentsang we came to know that two great Chinese Silk route passed through Central Asia and Majumdar; R. C. Hindu Colonies in Far East Calcutta 1963 Import of Chinese Silk was an important trade in ancient period. In Oman countries traders were highly paid for the Chinese Silk, so it must have tempted Indian trade and merchants. So Majumdar is near to truth. He further adds that no doubt other forces were at work to speed up the course of emigration. The missionary zeal of Brahman and Buddhist, pressure caused by increasing population, invasion of foreign tribes, and the spirit of adventure of Kshatriya princes and nobles were added to the commercial enterprises of the merchants. It is not clear when first migration of Indian people to the Central Asian territories took place, but from ancient documents we came to know that Khotan kingdom was established with the joint venture of Ashoka's son Kustana and his punished Prime minister. (Majumdar R.C. Hindu Colonies in Far East; Calcutta.")

1. GEOGRAPHY

As far as the Noman culture is concerned Central Asia is the name given to the largely deserted area triangular in shape, stretching from the eastern shores of the Caspian sen to the Great wall of China.

Geographically, it is divided by the Pamirs; the western part now under Russian domination comprises the ancient regions of Chorasmia and Sogdiana, and the eastern part now occupied by the Chinese, comprises the ancient kingdom of Khotan, Kucha, etc. collectively known as Ser India. The importance of Central Asia lies in the fact that 'from classical times to the Tseu of Marco Polo, it was the bridge of trade, religion, and culture that spanned the world between east and west' called as 'melting pot' by Bagchi. so, modern Russian Turkestan, Chinese Turkestan, and Tibet along with the inner part of Mongolia was the seat of ancient Central Asia, the Ser India of Stein ., where Indian cultural penetrated its roots in the 1st century A.D.

1. Heart Land of Asia, London 1977
2. Bagchi P.C. India and Central Asia, Calcutta 1955 p.14
3. Stein . A. Ser India 5 volumes.

The area is bounded by Tien Shan (a celestial Mountain) in the north and by the Kun Lun range in the south. Nan Shan, a continuation of Kun Lun bounds it in the east while the Pamirs, the ancient greek geographer, s imaos 'a link between Hindu Kush and Tien- Shan in the west. The area of Central Asia is roughly 1448 km. from the east to the west and its largest width, from Kucha in the North to the foot of Kun Lun range in the south of Niya, is roughly 383 km, the oases of Tumshuk, Kucha, Kara Shehr (Agni desh) and Turfan are situated on the north Silk Road. The Encyclopedia of discovery and exploration defines Central Asia as follows: 'Sandwiched in between Tibet and Siberia lies the Giant desert west of Central Asia. roughly triangular, it begins just east of Kashmir, with the Takakamakan.

Desert, and gradually widens out into a vast complex of waste Land that includes the Dzungaria, the ordos, and the mighty Gobi Desert of Central China and Mongolia. except for Its eastern fringes, the whole black region is enclosed and broken up by mountain ranges the Pamirs in the west, the Tien Shan, Altai, and Khingan in the north, and Kun- lung, Astin Tagh, and Nan Shan in the south.

1. Bhattacharya, c. Art of Central Asia 1977
2. Encyclopaedia. of discovery and exploration vol. 13 The heartland of Asia, Aldus book London. 1971.k London. 1971.

The mountainous range gives rise to important rivers that flow towards the Takalemaken desert, gradually dry up, and ultimately lose themselves in the sand. Tien Shan and Pamirs are sources of Kashgar Dariya and Yarkand Dariya respectively. Jointly they formed the Tarim River, which flows towards the marshes of lob nor. this is no other than the Suta River of Indian Literature. their banks were the seat of prosperous and thickly populated colonies in early times. in the southern part from west to east. cokkuka in the modern Yarkand, sallidesa in Kashgara, khotama godana in Khotan, and Ramadan in the church region. In the northern part too, from east to west flourished bhakura in modern uch Turfan, kuchirajya in the region of Kucha, and agnidesa in Karasahr. Through the Tarim basin from the frontier of China to the West important trade routes passed, also known as the Silk routes. Traders carried Chinese Silk via this route to roman countries in the west. racial conflict took place while controlling the Route, and for a few centuries since the Han period Chinese emperor Had to face a lot of trouble in guarding this rout of eastern Turkestan.

Two routes passed through the Tarim basin from the frontiers of China up to Balkh. from about the first century A.D., they were used not only for trade between China and the west but also for the dissemination of Buddhist culture from the west to the states of eastern Turkestan and China. later on, these were predominantly Buddhist routes and were used for cultural Exchange till about the 11th century A.D.

D. from Tunghuang in the province of Kansu two principal routes were bifurcated one passed by the gate of yu men kuan towards the north-western and the other by that of yang- kuan directly westward. Tunghuang played an important role in cultural exchange. in the later 2ndCentury Buddhist pilgrims found a place of shelter on their way to China. in the 3rd century A.D., we hear of Indian families settling down in Tunhuang, by the time it was a great center of Buddhist missionaries. when the Wei dynasty came to the throne, they determined to bring about a transformation of the place, important for the diffusion of Buddhist culture (as they were great patrons of Buddhism and Buddhist art). it was The time when construction of the Buddhist temple began and Grottos were multiplied until there were a thousand of them containing many works of art and statues of Buddha.

Tunghuang contained a large number of manuscripts, discovered mostly by the French archaeological mission of Pellot. it shows that during the Tang dynasty, it was a great center of learning. The manuscripts are in Kuchean, Khotan, Syriac, Tibetan, Sanskrit, etc. languages. It was a great center for meeting the East (China) and the west. The southern route starting from Tunghuang passed by the gate of Yang Kuen and proceeded west ward reach the Country of Shan Shan (to the south of Lob nor) from Shan Shan It went along the course of river Tarim up to so – Kiul (Yarakand) and crossed Pamir (Kizil Rabbet) reached to country of Ue Che (Balkh) and Nang- shi (Parthia). The route of the north passed by Kiue She (Turfan), the ancient capital of the kingdom of Lou-Lan, it followed the Tarim right upto the west of shu lei (Kashgara) and continued across the Pamir (Kizil) art upto the country of Taiwan (Ferganah) Kang Kiu (Sogdiana) and other countries in the valley of Oxus.

But the route of India followed a little different course. Fahien the first Chinese pilgrim to India, noticed in detailed the way He followed from China to India. starting from Changan in 399 A.D. with other monks passed by the principal localities of the province of Kan- -Su- viz. lan chou, leang Chou, Kan Chou, and tung Ho arrived at Shan- Shan to the south of Lobnor. they visited the countries of Yang-ki (Karashar), Yu Tien (Khotan), Tseu-Ho (Karaghalika), Kiuan Yu Mo (Tash Keoghan), and Kie Chia (Kashgar). They passed to toll (Darel, in Dardistan) and then, crossing the mountains reached the valley of Gilgit which leads to the region of the Indus. Riuan Tsang in 629 followed the northern route from Klan Su He went to Kao Cahng (Yarkhoto, near Turfan) then He visited the countries of A- ki- ni (Karasahar), Kiu- che (Kucha), po- lu- kia (Rarka Aryk) to the south of Tien Shan. He crossed the Tien-Shan by the Bedal pass and passed by the north bank of Issiqal, where He mates the Okmak Turks. Shortly before the arrival of Hiuan T Sang, the country was visited by an Indian monk of Nalanda Prabhakaramitra, who went to China later to receive the highest honor from the emperor of China.

The ancient Silk route had another section, the western one which connected the Roman Orient with Balkh during the early centuries of the Christian era. from Balkh it passed Antioch, the capital of Syria, through Heru, Hecatompylos (Raghes near Teheran) Eclanta (Ramadhan) and Hieropolis (Hen Bidi) on the Euphrates. The Persian empire, therefore, had a share in the silk trade with roman countries, and we have seen that this often brought her into conflict with central Asian nomads. but the cultural exchange between various nations. Almost a millennium along the Silk Route throws into back ground of their commercial interest.

PEOPLE

Central Asian can be bifurcated in pre-civilization and post-civilization. The people belonging to pre- civilization were mostly barbarous and they led a tribal life again they were of two groups (a) Nomadic and (b) Sedentary. From south Russia to Mancharia was inhabited by nomadic people while sedentary occupied the south including the oases of Eastern Turkestan. Scythians, Mongolians, Manchurians, Turco Mongols, and Buns were important Tribes

Day. Scythians included various tribes of Indo-European. Herodotus paints other tribes too i.e., sarmatiana massages, Arimaspes, isssedones, etc. Dr. Bagchi identifies them as follows;

(I) Saramatess neighbor of Scythians of South Russia.

(II) Massagetess massaygata fisherman spoke the Iranian language.

(III) Issedoness finno uggarian

(IV) Arimaspes lover of horses.

SCYTHIANS;

Social organizations

Scythians were like Iranians and three types of peoples such as warriors, priests, and agriculturists belonged to it. They had bad faith in the Zoroastrian religion, a primitive Indo-European religion. according to Herodotus, they worshipped Jupiter. The old Persian inscriptions speak of three different Tribes of these Scythians who were living in the north in the region extending from South Russia up to the central Asiatic Steppes they weres (1) Saka Haumavarke, who are more literally the Shakas of the Persian and Indian literature, settled in the region of farganah and extending upto Kashgar. (11) Saka tigrakhauda or Shakas with 'painted caps' spread towards the Aral and occupied the lower valley of Jaxartes. (111) Saka Taradraya, or Scythians who lived beyond the seas in south Russia. other races were the Sarmatians, massages, Arimaspes, biased ones, etc. mentioned by Herodotus.

The relics of ancient Scythian art and weapons who That they lived in a bronze age which continued in certain Areas till the 2nd century A.D. The easternmost center of this Culture was in Siberia in the upper valley of the Ienessel near Hinussink it was a metallurgical center that produced knives, daggers, cup eleven, cauldrons in bronze from the 5th century B.C to 3rd century A.D. These are relics of the Seytho Sarwathian culture which are to be found all over from inner Mongolia in the east of Hungary in the West.

1 Bagchi P.C. India and Central Asia cal 1955 P.S.

Although there had been earlier movements of the Scythian hordes from the Central Asia steppes to the west, The sedentary civilizations of China, Central Asia, Persia, and India do not seem to have been affected much by such movements before the 3rd century B.C. Since then, the movements became continuous till the times of the great Mongol invasions and affected the civilization of almost the whole of sedentary Asia. most of these race movements started in the Mongolian Deserts and set in motion all the nomadic tribes in the west.

As the Scythians of the north were nomads, we find no remains of their dwelling places, villages, or towns, but their burial places were built on a grand scale, and in them were buried many of their articles of daily use. it is from these burial places that we have been able to learn much about the life of Scythian tribes.1.

HUNS

The earliest of these movements was started in Mongolia by a people called Hiung nu in ancient Chinese History. Dr. Upendra Thakur has pained well to Hunas in his literary work Hunas in Ancient India". They were barbarous and nomadic. Chinese called them Hiung-nu. 2.
Sankrityana R. History of Central Asia. Cal. 1964, ixx p. 13.
Thakur; Hunas in Ancient India.......
Chinese were acquainted with them before the 3rd century B.C. when they lived in north China. Under the leadership of Shan-Yufuns were united at Qaraqurum in Mongolia. Chinese history

affirms that they were not Mongols but Turks based on their language and customs.

At the same time, China united under the great Tsin Emperor. Now, Hunas attacked China but they were uprooted from inner Mongolia by 210B.C. It is believed the Great Wall of China, one of the wonders of the world was the result of the Hunas' attack on China and it was built to check their depredations.

Hunas were not disheartened with defeat but they planned to attack and penetrate China through Kansu neither perfected by nature nor Human walls. The western part of Kansu was inhabited by Yu-ches, So, Hunas attacked them and was defeated in 176 B.C. Yu-che king was killed and the tribe was forced to leave Kansu with the death of Yu-che king. They disappeared like a seed of dehiscent fruit. But most of them advanced towards Nanshan in the south.

Defeat of the Yuches of Kansu made Hunas more powerful and these ants with wings wanted to touch the flames of the Chinese Lamp which was being organized under the wu-ti of handynasty.1.

1   Dr. Bagchi P.C.; Indian 7 Central Asia, cal. 1955 P.3.

Great Chinese Ho Kiu forced them to vacate Kansu. among the Hunas tribes Huensien and Kiu-chu Surrendered and accepted the vassalage of the Chinese in 121 B.C., this was not the Hunas attack. being droven from Kansu they joined the Louioan king near Lobnor but the king was punished for it.

Wu-sun was also a nomadic tribe living in the lli region Asked for help from the Chinese emperor against Hunas (71 B.C.)Turfan was also conquered for assisting Hunas by the Chinese in 67 B.C. and 65 B.C. Yarkand accepted Chinese sovereignty; Karasahar was also under Chinese dominion by 60 B.C. Hunas were now divided after the civil war for leadership Ho-han-, one of the claimants got Chinese patronage and became chief in 33 B.C. Che Che the other claimant moved west and defeated Wu- Sun in the lli region, Hukie of Imil, and Kien ku of the Aral region of Russian Turkestan and stopped at Tales region. But In 36 B.C. Chinese army killed Ho. Now, Hunas migrates to Europe. In 155 A.D. The Huna empire of Mongolia was destroyed by Sien-Pi (Sirbi), a Mongol horde. Sien-Pi advanced up to lli and defeated Wu-Sum in the course of a drive against Hunas. He extended from ''Manchuria up to Balkhash.1

1 Sankritayan R., History of Central Asia, cal. 1964 P. 9

Now, after defeating the Huns, they turned against the Chinese and conquered inner Mongolia in 156 A.D. and invaded Kansu. But Hunas were re-established in inner Mongolia to guard the frontiers at the beginning of 156 A.D. Hunas also affected the Gupta kings in India. Finally, they were driven out by Skanda Gupta.1.

YU-CHI

Yu-chi people were from the Tarim basin. Ancient Chinese records and archaeological remains from Central Asia show the position of the tribes in the Tarim basin i.e., Chinese Turkes-Tan. Aryan, a race allied to Yu-Chi were the expert or northern part of the Tarim basin, Kucha, Karasahr, up to western Kansu. They Spoke ancient Tokharian an Indo-European dialect of Wu-Sun a race allied to Yu-Chi were masters of the valley of the lli river in the region of the Balkash lake. The parts like Kucha, Karasahr, Turfan, and surrounding areas till the 8th century (when the Uigur invasion took place) were under Tukhara people, A branch of ancient Yu-Che.

Another Indo-European race, speaking the eastern Iranian Dialect was the occupant of southern oases of eastern Turkestan Kashgar, Yarkand, Khotan, Niya, lucullan (lob- nor region) up to Tunghuang.2.

Thakur, U; Hunas in Ancient India......

2 Bagchi P.C; India & Central Asia, cal. 1955 P.7. Herodotus speaks to this area as part of India. According to him "the part of India towards the rising sun is all sand, and that the country towards the east is a desert because of the sand. The desert people, according to him, were nomads, were raw flesh, and had Scythian customs regarding the disposal of their old men and women. India proper is distinguished by Herodotus as the country lying towards the South of Persia, bordering on Caspatyros (Kashmir), and Pactycal (Pakhta). The inhabitants, according to him resembled the Bactrians and were never subject to Darius. so Indo-European-speaking People occupied the entire Central belt of Central Asian including the area now called Chinese Turkestan right up to the Frontier of ex-China long before the 2nd century B.C.

TOKHARISTAN AND EASTERN IRAN

Tokharistan was the first country in Central Asia where Indian culture flourished. The place was named after the Tukharas, inhabitants of the region. Bagchi has painted it as a melting pot of various nomadic civilizations. It was the Tukhara people who carried the elements of Indian culture and religion to the North, and the East and transmitted to India the elements of the Iranian, Greek, and nomad cultures.1.

1 Bagchi P.C.; India & and Central Asia, cal. 1955 P. 20.

The geographical boundaries of Tokharistan in the 7th Century A.D. were as follows: -Sogdiana (modern Samarkand) in the North Hindukush or snow Mountains in the South, Persia in the west, and Pamirs in the East.

The river Oxus flowed through the country. Tokharistan was the Ta-Ho Chinese annals. According to Han Annals China first established contact with Ta-Ho in the 2nd Century B.C. Ramayana mentions them as Tukhara. Mahabharata and Buddhist texts i.e., Saddharmarityupasthana and Mahamayuri also accept it.

Tokharistan seems to have been under the rule of the Kushan till the middle of the 5th century. During the period 424-451 AD, a few merchants of Tokharistan went to the Chinese capital and taught the Chinese the secret of manufacturing polychrome Glass. The Kidara Kushans, even after their transfer to Balkh and Gandhara, sent embassies to China in 477 and 511. Kidara, and later his son, kungkas, waged war against the Sassanian king. Peroz (459 - 484). After the Hephthalite victory over Peroz, the Kidara Kushan under Kungkas moved to Kabul by the region, where they were later exterminated by the same hephthalites.1.

1 Bagchi P.C; India & Central Asia. 1955 cal. P. 24

TURKS

Chinese sources tell Turks as one of the Hun tribes. Which had been known in earlier times as the Ussena. In the Chinese accounts, Turks were mentioned as Tu-Kiu i.e., Turkut, which means strong. They were known in Indian literature as Turushka. They were descendants of the ancient Hiung-Nu race and had a wolf as their totem, and were living towards the beginning of the 6th century in the region of the Altai mountains as subjects of the Juan-Uans the Juan Juans became weak on account of a civil war between two chiefs A-Na-Kwei and his uncle, Po- Lomen (520), and although the former came out victorious and became the sole master of the Juan-Juans. Now, Po had to face the insubordination of his Turks vassals. In 433 A.D. The To-Ba Emperor tried to dispose of their territory and swallow up the tribe. at that time, 500 Ussena families fled to the Juan-Juan kingdom, where they worked as slaves, smelting iron in the Southern peaks of the Altai. As they wore pointed caps, they began to be called Dur-Po (Tu Pu, topi) which was later distorted into Turku. Turk, tyurok or turusk. The Turks had earlier lived in Iran, one of the culturally developed areas of China, but they do not seem to have benefited from it to any extent. However, as soon as the Juan-Juans were defeated, their chief, Tu-Min, declared himself free, and in about 546 A.D. He was proclaimed El-khagan. when Anakwe, the Juan-Juans king, refused to give his daughter in marriage to Tumin, He was killed by him.1 Ii khan is derived from El Khan Khakan. Khakan, Khagan, Khoman, and khan are all forms of Shanyu, which was the Chinese version of a word that in Hunnish was probably Chingis or Jing-Gis some have tried to distort this into Jungi it was the Juan-Juan who first adopted the little Khakan and later the word came to be used by the Turks as well as by Ho Mongols. Till 1917, the little Khan was reserved, in Central Asia, for kings alone, but in India, it had become almost valueless. Despite having carried in the beginning considerable weight. In earlier Tseu the designation Khan-khana had denoted a very high rank at the Mughal court in India, Akbar's protector and Prime minister Bairam khan, having been given this title but when the Mughal kings began to call themselves, shah, Shahenshah, or Padshah, the little Han began to lose its worth. Timur, the ancestor of Babar had reserved this title for his satellites and preferred to call himself Amir.

Tu-min was called Ii khan Tu-min it or el stands for the tribe and thus el-khan means king of the tribe. After assuming the title of el-khan, Tu-min began to distribute titles to others, During the time of the Huns the queen had been Called Yeng-Chi: now He was given the little Kho-Ho-tun, which Later became Kho-Tun, or Khotan.2.
Bagchi P.C. India & Central Asia cal. 1955 p. 19
Sankrityan R; History of Central Asia, cal. 1964 p. 43.
to this day in India, Muslim ladies of high rank are given the title of Khotan, during the lifetime of Tumin Turkish. Power had grown considerably and when he died in march 553 A.D. His tribe, known amongst the Chinese as Tu Kyu or Tui Ky Had won a name for itself.
Some of the important titles among the Turks were De le (te-le, Mongol, de re) prince, Kui-Lui-Chui (Khilich or Khilij), a Po (a pe), Ghe-Re-Phe (Sya-Li-Pha), Tu-Tun, Ji- Gin (Su Chin), etc. all indicating persons of high rank. In giving names the Turks try to describe the Qualities of the person e.g., she vau li yo, which means brave or powerful; san-de-lo, meaning fat; De-Lo-Biyan, one who drinks too much.

CULTURE

The Turks embrace Buddhism quite easily. The religion had a powerful influence over their lives until their conversion to Islam. This was their national faith, as it still is with the Mongolian people. However, their faith did not interfere with many of their national customs. e.g., that of placing the corpse in front of the dead man's tent where each one of his children's grandchildren, and other kinsmen would come and present a horse or a sheep.1.

1.Sankritayan R; History of Central Asia, cal. 1964 ivid.

Grief was expressed by the slashing of a face with a knife so that the tears mixed with blood. corpses were buried in the spring of autumn. Stones were set up on the graves as symbols of mourning and the number of stones placed on the grave denoted the number of the enemy slain by the dead warrior. On that day all the members of the family were dressed in the best robes and ornaments and if any woman caught the fancy of any of the men present a marriage proposal was sent to the girls' parents it was customary to accept such proposals. A similar custom was also current among the Syan-Pi.

The Huns had their pastures, which were situated on the Tu Chin Mountains, like the puns again they visited their pastures every year and offered sacrifices in honor of their ancestors. The whole tribe would collect at the time of these sacrifices; which were preferred during the period of a waxing moon, a hundred and fifty miles to the West of Tu-Chin stood Pu-Tengwi, a barren mountain. according to the Chinese, the Turkish alphabet was Ho(Suriyani), but they had no calendar.

The Turkish menfolk were fond of Tseu, while women played a kind of football. Their favorite drink was Koumiss which was a fermented liquor prepared from mare's milk.1.

1. IBID.

NATURE OF CONTACT:

It was Buddhism due to which India came into contact with other parts of the world. according to p.c. Bagchi Buddhism was the predominant religion in the various states of Tokharistan of the 2nd century B.C. up to the Beginning of the 8th century when it was conquered by the Arabs.1. So, at least in the 2nd century B.C. India must have come into contact with Central Asia and the nature of contact was religion i.e., Buddhism. Huan-Tsang, the great Chinese Traveller, and master of law, pointed out that Trapusa and Bhallika were responsible for introducing Buddhism in the Country and no doubt they were the first two lay disciples of Buddha 2. As He narrates: - "there were two merchants, natives of the kingdom of Bhalika. probably the name of one of themBhalluka or Bhallika is connected with the name of one country.

They had gone to India for trade and happened to be at Bodh Gaya when the Buddha had just attained his enlightenment. They offered him cake and honey and became his first disciples.3.

1. Bagchi; P.C. India and Central Asia; cal. 1955 p. 31
2. Waters; On Yuan Chwang 2 vols.
3. Ibid.

Legends continue to tell us that at the time of their departure, Lord Buddha gave them his hair and nail outings on their return home they built stupas on these relics Fiuan-Tsang mentions these stupas in the neighbourhood of the city of Bulkh. Whatever the legend, there seems to be no doubt that Buddhism was carried to Bulkh in the time of Ashoka. Asoka speaks of his efforts to introduce Buddhism among the people of Gandhara, Kamboja, and Yona in the following words: Gandhara were the people belonging to the Gandhara region of Central Asia.3 Kambojas were probably a branch of the Tukhara people. The Yona was no doubt the Greeks of bacteria it is not known what progress Buddhism made after its first introduction. but soon after Asoka, Demetrius, in conjunction with Menander, seems to have taken up arms in the defense of Buddhism, and its authorities and patrons, the descendants of Ashoka. The great Yue-Ches also, after their conquest of Tokharestian, adopted this new faith. The katanas became great patrons of Buddhism.

As B.G. Gafurou reported the conferences on the history, archaeology, and culture of Central Asia in the Kushan period, held in 1968 in Dushanbe, the capital of the Tajik soviet socialist republic, under UNESCO auspices, under the article

Bagchi; p.c. India & Central Asia; cal. 1955; p. 32 (2) & 3. Ibid.
''Kushan civilization and world culture'- ''It was in Kushen that Mahayana Buddhism received Its peculiar development, becoming widespread in counties of Central Asia and the far-east, Indian culture and art Penetrated this country. 1. So if we believe in Gafurov, as a word then have to accept that both forms of Buddhism i.e. Binayana and Mahayana prevailed in Central Asia

and the Buddhist missionaries from India were able to establish a relationship between India and Central Asia.

Gokhale comes forward to accept this "in China, Central Asia, and Tibet, the expansion of Indian culture was carried on Mostly through the Buddhist missionaries."2 He further added; - "In Central Asia, Indian traders, and missionaries frequently in Travelled through the princiPalities and with them spread the Influence of ancient Indian culture".3 in these lines He tells that trade was another factor for the spread of Indian culture in Central Asia. as we know that there was

1. Central Asia in the Kushan period vol I. Moscow 1974. p. 77. Proceedings of the international conferences on the history, archaeology, and culture of Central Asia in the Kushana period.
2. Ancient India; B.G. Gokhale; cal. 1962 p. 207
3. Gokhale BG Ancient India cal 1962 p. 208.

A regular trade relationship between India and China in the ancient period. and through Central Asia passed the great trade routes connecting India with China 1, and along this route spread Indian ideas and customs. Kashgar, Yarkend, Khotam, and Kuchi became important centers of Buddhism and Buddhist monasteries soon dotted the Central Asia landscape. In Khotan lay the great Buddhist establishment of "Gomati" which was a center of learning. According to the Chinese travelers, the monks of Kuchi know Sanskrit well and the Buddhist teachers of Kuchi played a great role in the spread of Buddhism in China from the 3rd to the 5th century A.D.

Like Kuchi, in Turfan also many Buddhist monks were engaged in the work of translating religious books into Tokharish, and both Fashien and Huen-Tsang were received with great respect and hospitality. Scholars who believe in trade relationships as a factor for the contact between India and Central Asia present the pages From Ptolemy's Geography. The main overland route between India or the west and China passed through Central Asia.

1 Gokhale; B.G.; Ancient India; cal. 1962; p. 209
Many colonies grew up in these river valleys. people of Kashmir and north-western India started colonies in Khotan and Kashgar in the first two centuries A.D.

2. ROUTE

Trade was one of the factors for the expansion of Indian Culture into Central Asia. Chang-Kien the Chinese general and explorer of Central Asia in the 2nd century B.C. testified that there was a trade relation between north-eastern India and south-western China. From China, Chinese Silk cloth and Chinese Bamboo, flutes among other things were brought into Eastern India and were carried through the entire length of North India up to Afghanistan and Central Asia.

S.K. Chatterjee states that Indo-Mongols were the intermediaries in this trade. It may be conjectured that these Indo-Mongoloids included both the people of India and Nepal. From the accounts of Yuan-Chuang, the Tang Annal, and other sources we know that the continuous flow of commerce in the over land trade route from Bihar to Tibet and China through Nepal has also been conjectured.

In 1538, R. Fitch noticed that trade between Nepal, Bhutan, and Tibet and the caravan of merchants coming from China, Mongolia, Tatary, and Persia. The detailed description of an interesting ledger of an American merchant named Hovhannes Joughyetsi gives a pen picture of the commercial link between India, Nepal, and Tibet in the closing decades of the 17th century. The narration of father Della Penna a British merchant and Fippdict Desideri in the early 18th century also confirmed that the course between India and Tibet via Nepal was unrestricted. flourishing trade was carried on between India and Tibet through the passes of Nepal. The Kasmir merchants carried their goods by Ladakh to the Kuti passes to procure wool from there. From this point their manufactured goods were sent partly to Tibet and Partly to China by Sining (a town situated on the Chinese Border, and partly to Patna through Nepal.

the Tibetan merchants brought woolen clothes, ponies (a kind of fruit), shawls, goats, yaks, sheep, musk (teeth of an elephant), salt, bronze, Gold, silver, and paper to Kathmandu. The lamas of Tibet Also sent much bullion to Nepal mints. The Indian merchants carried cotton clothes, cutlery, glassware, coral, pearls, Spices, camphor, beetle, and hardware. these were sent to Tibet through the passes of Nepal.

George Bogle in his letter dated 20th august, 1774 informed Warren Hastings that the trade between India and Tibet was carried on by the way of Patna and Nepal through Means of Moghuls and Kashmiris. Subsequently, in his report on the trade in Tibet. He further stated that the Merchants of Kashmir like Jews in Europe or Americans in the Turkish Empire scattered themselves over the eastern kingdoms of Asia and carried on expensive trade between its distant parts.

They disposed of their commodities in Tibet or forwarded them to their associates in Shining. he commodities or Bengal were also conveyed to Tibet through Morug (a place situated in Nepal) and Sikkim. Besides this, another road is added from Banaras and Mirzapur passing through Mus-Tang (a place in Nepal).

The more valuable kinds of Bengal goods were sometimes exported into Tibet by this route. Thus, it is evident that the trade between India and Central Asia was carried on freely before the ascendancy of the Gorkhas in Nepal in 1769. Since then the trade sharply declined. The geography of Ptolemy also helps us to search for trade relations between India and Central Asia. Bunbury also accepts that the overland route between India or the West and China passed through Central Asia. Many colonies grew up in these river valleys. People of Kashmir and North-Western India started colonies in Khotan and Kashgar in the first two centuries.1

1. E. H. Bunbury; cf.; History of Ancient Geography; p. 486- 7

Another route passed from Taxila center which ran along the valley of Kabul River, passed by Hadda and Nangarhar (Jalalabad), and reached Bamiyan, a valley surrounded by snowy cliffs of the

Hindukush. The crossing of the Hindukush thin route reached Bactrian (modern Balkh) were covered almost all the great trade-routes of Central Asia.1Rich sources of revenue to the state and wealth to the people was India's relation with the outside world. As far hack as the 7th century, we have evidence of India, 's Maritime relations with the middle eastern world as indicated by baveru jataka. There was a regular trade relationship between India and China.

INLAND ROUTES

Balkh was at the junction of two great highways of Central Asia to China, the northern, and the southern. The Northern route passed through ancient Sogdiana2, crossed the Jaxartes, passed by Tashkent, went west wards through the Passes of the Tien-Shan, and at last reached Ucha-Turfan. The other, shorter passed through the country of Tokharians;

1. Chakravarthy, h; trade & commerce of ancient India cal p. 39.

2. Stein , Khotan; London; 1907. P. 52

From sule (Kashgar) the Road passing westward across the Tsung-ling mountains goes on to Ta-wan, Khang-chu, and Yang Tsai country, the regions which were long ago identified with the ancient Sogdhians."

Near Balkhan and over the difficult passes of Pamirs, reached the plain at Kashagar with the upper valley of the Indus. It passes through the Gilgit and the basin valleys up to Tash Kharghan, where it joins the other route proceeding towards Kashgar1.

Kalhana's Rajtrangini shows the mountains routes corresponding to the modern Gilgit transport road i.e., routes from Volur lake to the valley of Gurez, A. Stein has shown the character and historical importance of the old watch station or Gates of Kashmir in his "memoir on the ancient geography of Kashmir. Three important routes have been pointed out by Ptolemy which ran from Sogdhiana to the source of the Oxus and Jaxartes (1) the

Southern route ascended the high valley of Oxus through Badakhshan (II)the Central one ran straight to The Kashgar by the high valley of Jaxartes and (III) the northern One went down a part of middle valley of the Jaxartes And then turned to the east towards the Chinese territory.2

The relationships between Central Asia and India became closer under the Kushans whose existence in Bharatawarsa1 is proved as early as 64 A.D. by the Panjtar record. As we know the Kushans took advantage of the weakness of the Parthian kingdom in northern western India, entered into India, and established a mighty empire extending from Oxus valley to the Banaras, in the east.

1.   Bagchi P.C; India and China; P. 13

2.   Ptolemy's geography; ed. Mc Crindle. P.12.

The relationships between Central Asia and India became closer under the Kushans whose existence in Bharatawarsa1 is proved as early as 64A.D. by the Panjtar record. as we know that the Kushans took advantage of the weakness of the Parthian kingdom in northern western India, entered into India and established a mighty empire extending from Oxus valley to the Banaras. In the east. Kanishka extended his sway in Central Asia up to the borders of the Yellow River and sent him, the royal princess as a hostage2. Panchao, the Chinese general began by this time his campaign westward and naturally came to clash with Kanishka. Levi's summary of the Chinese account of Panchao, 's campaigns may be quoted here ''Panchao's victorious campaigns pursued for 30 years (73-102 A.D.) without interruption at this very time restored Siyu (the west) to the empire and carried Chinese arms beyond the regions explored by Chang-Kien, as far as the confines of the Greeco-roman world. By 73 A.D. The kings of Khotan had made his submission; several kings of that country followed his examples and gave their eldest sons as hostages for their fidelity. Kashgar, immediately after, returned to obedience. The two passes by which the way to the south debouches into India was in the hands of the

Chinese emperor the Yuchi had not renounced their previous supremacy without a struggle. In the year 90, the kings of Yue-chi sent an ambassador to demand a Chinese princess in marriage. Panchaos, deeming the request insolvent, stopped the ambassador and sent him back. The king of Yue-Chi raised an army of 70,000 equestrians under the order of the viceroy Sie. Sie was vanquished and the king of the Yue-Chi did not fail to send every year the tributes imposed upon him.

1. India was well known at that time as Bhartavarsa.

Waters; on Yuan Chwang, 1. p. 124.

Panchaos, deeming the request insolvent, stopped the ambassador and sent him back. The king of yue-chi raised an army of 70,000 horsemen under the order of the viceroy sie. she was vanquished and the king of the yue-chi did not fail to sent every year the tributes imposed upon him. The yue chi king referred to here appears to be no other than kaniska who was evidently defeated by the Chinese general. hence, we see that Panchao established his supremacy over Central Asia and extended the Chinese power up to the Caspian Sea. Khotan and Kashgar submitted to the Chinese armies in 73 A.D. and the southern route was known open to commerce. With the submission of Ku Che and Kashgar in 94 A.D. commerce by the northern route was regularly carried on between east and west2 of course, trade by this route was

1. Indian Antiquaries: p. 421-2; 1903.

2. Washington; Commerce p. 87; Schoff ed. of the peri P. 268.

Opened up only nominally, the savage still being powerful there. Trade flourished by this route under the roman emperor Marcus Aurelius (169-180A.D.). In ''Ser India''; Stein points out two possible roads one, the mountain route, longer but practicable throughout the year passed along the high barren slopes of the Kunlun range i.e. Altiq-tag, and the other, the desert route began winding round the Karakoshan merges and ran along the south of salt-lake bet to reach the center of the oasis of Tung-Huang towards eastern Turkestan. The Northern route leading to Tolou-lan was the most popular probably first laid by the Chinese to get easy and direct access to the great northern string of Oases. Stein came across "the white dragon mounds" on this route, used to cart-traffic from Tung Huang westwards during the first few centuries after Christ. The Wei-llo tells us three routes from Tung-Huang to the western countries. Two routes of the south and the center are said to have passed along the Altiq-Tagh slopes to Miran and through the desert to Lou-Lan respectively; whereas the north is mentioned to have started from Yu-Men-Kuan, passed through avoiding the San Lung desert and reached Chushit at Kao-Chang (Turfan) and the turning west, must have re-joined the Central route at Chiutzu (Kucha). The former Han annals speak of this new route of north- "during the period of Yua- Nashin (1 - 5A.D.) was made a new route which, passing north of Wu-Chian penetrated as far as the Yumen barrier." Chavannes thinks that this route was opened in the 2nd A.D. Only to reduce the distances and avoid the white dragon mounds. Stein also thinks that the complete reduction of Lou-Lan in 77 B.C. was followed by the institution of a Chinese protector-general in 60 B.C. only to control both the routes of the north and south.1 it is interesting to note here that Stein found a valuable relic at the station ixv of the ancient skill trade.

1. Stein .; Ser India chapter XIV. P. Central 548.

The relic consists of two strips of fine Silk undyed (t. xv. 111 57), with an inscription"(ai) St. Asia pata gis. ti saporisa", which proves beyond doubt that between 61 B.C. and 9 A.D., traders used the Indian language and script to travel by this route across the Chinese lines for the Silk of the seres2. The line of the limes ceased to work by the middle of the 2nd century A.D., when of course, the Lou-Lan route linking Tun-Huang with China continued its use. The house amid the sand-buried ruins of Lop nor, where a small bale of silk was found to be perfectly preserved, bears clear testimony to the use of this route by traders of the period of our investigation.

Thus, the number of colonies planted by Indians on the both the routes,

1 ibid P. 730

2 ibid P. 701-703.

Thus, the numbers of colonies planted by Indian on the both the routes, north and south of the Tarim basin speak of the use of the three routes from very early times. Kashagar, Yaskan, Khotan, Niya (smaller pieces of coloured rug found in the old site beyond the Niya River) (given in the plate (LXXV)2, their swastika like pattern and stupa like ornament; their origin in India and establish her trade-relation along with this route), and many others on the southern route contributed much to the trade and cultural relationship between Central Asia and western countries i.e. India.

1 ibid P. 733.

3. SOCIETY (including religion and philosophy)

It is a universal truth that whenever an inferior Culture comes in contact with a superior one it grasps the elements of a superior culture, the same is the case with Central Asian people. Even the tribes that attached to Indian Territories and ruled over some part of it gradually vanished in the Indian society. We hear of Shaka, Kushanas, Huns, and other tribes ruling in India during the 1st century A.D. Till the death of the great Gupta king Skanda Gupta. But after Gupta's rule, we have no trace of the separate existence of these tribes in Indian society.

The Indian authors who established their culture in Central Asia were mainly based on their lives in India. Niya, Kucha, Turfan, Khotan, etc. were the important seat of Indian culture in Central Asia. It was about 70 years ago that Sir A. Stein discovered about 764 Kharosthi documents on wood, Silk, leather, and Paper, at Niya, Endere, and Loulan in Chinese Turkistan. These are written in the Kharosthi script which was the most popular in north west part of India during the early centuries of the Christian era. Their language is Prakrit which is popularly designated as the Niya Prakrit after the type site Named ''Niya'' in the Tarim basin of Chinese Turkestan. Later on, 18 of such documents were edited by Dr. J. Burrow1 (BSOAS London, IX, PP 111 125), thus raising their total number to 782.

These documents from Central Asia have got an important beam on the life and culture of people in these distant regions during the first three centuries of the Christan Era. They bear ample testimony to the existence of Indians in the heart of Chinese Turkestan during the contemporary period; they were then using an Indian script and also on Indian dialect with some impact of the Iranian Language. The above sites fell on the ancient Silk route connecting China with the western world as well as India. Merchants and traders from far-flung countries moved from one side to the other in search of foreign goods. This had some impact on their languages and cultural life as well. The previously mentioned site of Chinese Turkestan has also yielded several coins, on one side of which we find legends in the Kharosthi script whereas the other side bears Chinese letters. They are called Sino Kharosthi coins. It is evident that

----

1 BSOAB; London; ix PP 111-125.

although Indians formed the most powerful group in contemporary Society, they were living with the Chinese, Iranians, and the local people in a spirit of harmony in these regions and that is why they felt the necessity of introducing a common Currency that served the needs of all the groups.1

Most of these Kharosthi documents are of a secular Nature. Some of them are royal messages, personal letters, Court deeds, and state archival material. We have not so far come across such early records in Indian territory and as such the former are a valuable source of information about the Indian way of life, in the heart of Central Asia, during the pre-Gupta period.

SYSTEM OF GOVERNMENT

The Kharosthi documents prove beyond doubt that sovereignty rested with the king who was usually designated as Maharaya (Skt. maharaja). He was addressed in a very eloquent manner, State injunctions and letters, in Kharosthi Script. As referred in a series of charming titles and epithets for him such as Maharayasa Rayatirayasa Mahamtasa Jevamatasa, Dharamiasa Sachadhamastidasm Pruchahadovada Nuava Maharaya Deva Putrasa (No. 655)2. a number of them appear on the Kushan coins as well; righteous as the king was a "deity incarnates". The queen was called devi, while the king's son as Maharaya-putra1. proper record of the state officials (Raji Jamna) has been also maintained. proper record of the state officials (Raji Jamna) has also been maintained. The document may frequent References to the army people (Seniye Jamna) in connection the document may frequent references to the document may frequent references to

----

1. Buoyer A.M.; et al, Kharosthi inscription .... Oxford;

   Vols. I- III, 1920- 29

2. as indicated on documents by archaeologists.

The document frequently refers to the army people (Seniye Jamna) in connection with the protection of high ways from robbers and enemies because there was frequent danger from the"Supiyas".

A regular system of administration was evolved where various departments were entrusted to different high officials. We have got very interesting glimpses of the state injunctions and letters of command in these documents. Such as Anathi or Anadi or Anada Lekha, corresponding to Ajnptilekhas or Ajnapatras described in Indian literature. These were duly sealed as is evident from the availability of actual sealed-wedge-shaped tablets and designated as Anati- Kilamumdra (skt. Kilamudra). every care was taken to incorporate relevant detail in the official correspondence; Confidential letters were sent through a special messenger (cara-purusha in No. 310). The letter began with the common phrase Mahamanava Maharayalihati and then followed the Epithets of the next high official followed by his actual name. sometimes there was even a reference to the frequent reminders having been sent to a certain official. The king believed in piety and judgment in accordance with religion1. In the words of A. Stein ''official custom also a style for less ornate is amply shown by the business and Peremptory tone adopted in some of the wedge-shaped tablets, Ordering submissions of affidavits according to a specified list, production of certain witnesses, arrest of certain individuals, c."2

---

1. Niya document no. 622, 634.

At the time of political upheaval and impending attempt from the enemies, secret communications were made through Vinatilekhas, most perhaps corresponding to the Pravartika letters in Indian literature the Kharosthi documents using the word 'Suta or Dutiya' for an ambassador furnish very interesting information about their appointment and functions the state took every care in rendering all sorts of help to such dignitaries

---

1. Dhamen nice Kartave NO. 1

2. Stein A; Ancient Khotan; Oxford' 19 P. 367.

A fact which is daily confirmed from contemporary literature as well.

SOCIAL LIFE

The documents, under review, also throws a flood of Light on the life of common folk. The system of salavery was very much prevalent, even the Buddhist monks could well afford to deal in the sale and purchase of the slaves. The words used for slaves (skt. dasas may be enumerated as Tseu, Dajha, Dhaja, Dajhajana for a male slave while Tseu, Dajhi denoted a female slave (Skt dasi). The master was addressed as Bhatara (skt. bhattarka).

There were porters (prthabharige in No. 376 skt. Prakha Thareka) for carrying goods. Regular use of animals for distant journey was made and check posts established to provide rest and relation on the way. The employee was entitled to receive food and clothing for staying in the herds, in strict accordance with the law (oodaga-paohevara parikraya davo; No. 194); the slaves received food (Bhata) and clothing(codaga) whereas the guards were paid in the form of corn (No. 476). According to document No. 591, the purchaser of a man is entitled to sell, to pledge, to exchange, to give to other as present and even to do whatever He likes with the latter. The sale agreement was duly registered to this effect.

A few Kharosthi documents, under review, are nothing else but actual documents which informed about important portion of state archives in Niya region.

FAMILY LIFE

The Kharosthi documents from Chinese Turkistan have got an important bearing on the Hindu family system when they refer to purely Indian terminology in daily use such as Purusa (male persons), Pitu, pita for father, Matu, Madu etc. for Mother; Putra and Suta for son Pitumaha for grand father Prapotra for Praoutra for grandson; Napata for grand son; Bhrata, Bhratu for brother, Bhrata-putra for brother's son

Imata for son-in-law; Syasu for sister, Bharya for wife, Putriddhuti for daughter etc. The use of Panjabi words as India and Kudi for a male and female child respectively, is equally interesting. Indian words as Kula and Parivar are also available. The Niya document appears to refer a patriarchal society. Wherein father used to command great respect. The birth of a son was deemed to be an occasion of great rejoicing and happiness.1 The son had very beautiful epithets for his father during correspondence,1 from this it is evident that the father was held in great esteem. besides this, there was a common belief of 'a life-span of one hundred years and that is why in some documents, the son has addressed his father as Satay-Upramanassa. this may very well be compared with the Indian Motto may be live and hear for hundred years. Life was not a burden to people in the contemporary world.

----

1 Niya document No. 702- Putra-Jata Savahr Satanabhavitavya.

Central Asian society which was dominated by Hindu thought and culture. One of these Kharosthi documents 3 even states that all creatures, on entering doctrine of the Tathagatas, mark of birth and death a great emphasis was made on the performance of the noble actions and leading a chaste life. Even the ruler was expected to abide by law (dharma)- a fact which is very well corroborated by the epithet Soadhamastidasa for a king, in several document under review. Brahma Charita. there was frequent sale and purchase of girls which appears to have been a local trade of the Niya society.

1.. Priyadarsana Deva- Manush- Sampujitasa Pichara Divyavarsa Shayuoramanasa Priya-Pitu

2. Jivem sharadah shatam, shrunuyam shardahatam.

3. Niya document no. 511

4. Niya document no 399 Sampraja Kartavya Kujal Kartavya Brahma Charita.

this was an Indian practice. The society was missed containing not only the Hindus from India but also the locally born people.

VIEW ON RICHNESS

From Niya document the unstable nature of prosperity and riches in very beautiful words, and idea which has only Frequently quoted in Indian literacy texts as well. According to documents number 5 to 3" just as a man travelling on jour-Ney rest here and thee whenever overcome by fatigue, so a Man's riches having rested from time to time, come back again Yatha Manusiya Pathi

Vartamanah Kvacit Kvacit Visramats Sramarttah Tatha Manusyasya Dhanani Kale-Kale Smmasvasya Punar Brajanti the same document further refers to a prayer for Victory and prosperity.2

1.Niya document no 5 to 3

2. Sata subhichu bhavatu samakula imiram vivridhi abhi varsatu Makhi udemtu sasya ca jayaya parthiva ciram Sadhamasugatatisthatu.

VIEW ON KNOWLEDGE

Niya documents allude to a person anxious to gain Proficiency in several branches of knowledge such as grammar, (sabda) music (Gandharva), happening on earth and in air (bhumi vata) carida), astronomy (jotisa), poetry (kavya karmana), Dancing talave painting (citragaram abhirajate), e t c. references to twelve Nakshatras in Kharosthi document no. 565 is equally interesting.

MATERIAL CULTURE

The Kharosthi documents from Chinese Turkistan present enough data relating to the material culture of contemporary Niya region. Stora, pasu, and jamdu (Skt. jantu) denoted an animal in general camel mostly used for transport and carrying goods from one place to another, was called uta (Skt. ustra) In addition to about two dozen epithets used for the same animal in general came mostly used for transport and carrying goods from one place to another was called uta (skt. ustra) in addition to about two dozen epithets used for the same Animal. Horse was equally popular as is evident from the use of the word apsa (skt. asva) and vadavi (skt. vadva for the Mare. These are references to a pregnant cow (go ghabhina2), a large cow (go mahatma in number 122), calves of cows (gavisvtse3, royal cows (narbak gavijana4), and cow enclosure5. etc.

----

1. no. 514

2. no 186

3. no 7

4. no 159

5. go adamant)

other animals enumerated in these documents mariga(deer)khar (ass), suna (dog skt. svana) lomatic (for hindil lomdi skt. Lomatka); lion is addressed as kesan (no. 103), vyagra (no.565), simgha (no. 511). The animals were a regular source of supply of meat to the people in general and to the military in particular they were frequently gifted away between individuals, served as means of transport for distant journeys on the sandy high-ways of Central Asia, provided wool and leather for day to day uses etc. the discovery of few Kharosthi documents on leather pieces is all the more interesting, the society allowed the use of leather for writing purposes while chama-pothi in document No. 17 refers Tao book prepared from leathers (Carsa Pustaka). The use of the Indian word pothi is equally interesting

LAND AND AGRICULTURE

The Niya document refers to an Indian terminology in this direction as well. Bhuma, Buma, and Bhumi denoted land (kst Bhumi) in general. other terms have been used for specific and such as arable land (Bhuma-Chetra or Bhum Chitra), farm land (gotha bhunio) sandy land (sigata bhuma) waste land (vyarta bhumi No. 713) e t c. The king had his lands and villages, royal grounds were usually made in favor of the fugitives and slaves. private lands wee freely sold, purchased, and given in exchange to other persons, and deeds were duly recorded to that Effect.

Most of the Kharosthi documents are in the form of land deeds, and court decisions in case of disputes about their sale, transfer, and policy of wonder ship. The documents throw some light on the marking of boundaries, sowing, plowing, etc. Spring (vasanta) was considered as Suitable season for cultivation purposes (vasantmani) caramans, No 450) as also in ancient China. The Niya people believed that plowing, sowing, and tilling of vines yards if conducted in the pig nakshatra, were sure to be successful and fruitful (sugra nakshatra vavanamasu sada uchavina sidhi vardhi bhavi-Syati No. 565). Water was regarded as the back bone of irrigation and it was diverted from one channel to the Other for irrigation purposes, thus indicating the existence of a well-planned irrigation system in contemporary society1. The documents record the use of the bhajan, biji, bhisa, etc for Seed (Skt. biji).

TAXATION

The system of taxation was quite elaborate in the Niya society. taxes could be paid in the form of corn, farm products, liquids such as ghee and wine, animals such as camels, textiles, and garments such as blankets, carpets, felt, etc. The documents present a vivid record of taxes and demand lines in arrears and reminders having been issued to that effect, asking the address to forward the current year's taxes along with those of the previous years (No. 165). There was no exemption of taxes in times of famine and drought. Only a few privileged persons could enjoy some concessions and commissions, including the grant of royal Tseu (Rayaka Harga) from a particular locality and, the award of corn and land free from military tax. The state had appointed several officials for the taxation departments, proper record of the taxpayer and taxes paid from time to time was dully maintained there was frequent security of the taxes lying in arrear taxes collected in various kinds.

Kr. sivatrami udaga nasty audak huta, ahuno Tseu rijammi

nivartyavidavya no 125).

camels were usually employed for transporting wine, and corn. collected as tax from various sources. Most of the Kharosthi documents from Chinese Turkestan, related to such matters are disputes arising there. Some of these documents are written on wooden takhatis (wooden beards) which are so often used by school children in India even now a Tseu. The shape of the takhli in Central Asian records, appears to have been derived from Indian takhti. A Graphic depiction of the same, but dates back to the Shunga period is to be seen on a tiny terra cotta plaqe from (Shugha Haryana) and is now preserved in the National Museum at New Delhi1. A boy is shown learning the vowels appearing in the contemporary Brahmi script on this interesting terracotta plaque; The shape of a takhti placed between the legs of the child; bears

----

1. Central Asian gallery, national museum No. 60,193.

The close resemblance with the wooden takhtis from Chinese Turkestan. A some what similar type of takhati has been excavated from the Site of Taxila as well.

PERSONS AND PROFESSIONS

The phrase kammakarejamma reminds us of one of the karmaka used by Panini (3.2.22) in the sense of an unskilled worker, engaged in manual work. other categories, enumerated in these Central Asian documents, included a sculpture (solpiga), carpenter (dacchamna or tacchamaa = skt. taksna), potter (kualaskt kulaba) bowmaker (dhamnukara), arrowmaker (kada karaskt kandakara), goldsmith (subarnakara), etc.

They also refer to the residents of different regions of Central Asia itself, i.e. persons hailing from Krorayena, chadota, Khotan, Siulika, etc. The Chinese merchants have been describing as cash Andevamiye1 while some persons were named after their Countries names as cinika, cinasena, cinapriya, cinaphara, Vinaya sa, Sena, priya and yasa ending names bear testimony to the impact tants of Indian culture on Chinese personal names in Niya society, such examples are numerous, one has only to read these documents carefully and collect them.

FOODS AND DRINKS

In relation to food and drinks of the people in Central Asia, we find a frequent reference to Indian works such as Bhata (rice) tamandula (rice) phalophala (fruit), pomegranate (dadima)bhoyamna (skt. bhajanas) spices as pepper (maricha), small cardamons (susmala), ghee (ghrida, ghrda) wheat and barely are denoted by gohomi (or godhuma) and yavi(yava), respectively. The phrase ghritakumbha suggest that ghee bored in storage jars as in India even now a Tseu.

TEXTILE AND GARMENTS

Mention may also be made of a number of Indian words in relation to textile and garments described in the document from Chinese Turkestan urna and samana denoted wool and hemp respectively pata has been interpreted to mean "a roll of silk." a first century A.D. Silk fragment from Tun-Huang bears the Brahmi inscriptions referring to the length of the particular roll of the silk as 46 gistis or distis. a variant of pata, in the form of pada, occurs in a Kharosthi note on a silk stripe found in the Lopnor region of Chinese Turkestan. The use of patas in India has been alluded to in the Nagahara cave inscription of the Nayanika district was an equivalent of one span i.e., 9 inches of height. Chama or charma denoted leather. Some Indian color names also figure in these documents such as space (white), pandura (white or yellow), pita (yellow), nila(blue) raga(red), nilagm rataga (red-blue), ass color (khara varna), etc. kojya was used in the sense of rug (Pali, kojava). Veda for a turban (of China veda) cottage for upper garments, Kamali or kanjuliya for the bodice (skt kanchulika) Raju or rasamna for rope, gone for 'sack' etc.

COINS AND MEASUREMENT

Besides several Persian and Greek coins, we find references to the Indian currency maska as well, such as masa in the number 661 and masa in no.149 and 500 Suvarna and kanska denoted 'gold' in general. Besides disti (span), there was the system of measuring textile goods by hand (hasta Hindi hatha=18 inches) as also in India the height of human beings was usually recorded in dithis or tithis, a 'span' (skt. disti) land was measured by the number of seed it required for cultivation purposes. The document further refers to Indian words as half (adha), and quarter (pada) while the quantity is indicated by the word matra (Skt. matra)

RELIGION

Buddhism was very popular in the Niya region, the document refers to a Buddhist monk as sramana, samana, thesa, sthaira for sthavira, bhighu, bhuchu, ghichu for Bhikshu and Brahmin. For Brahmin, the Buddhist monks were leading a very rich life, possessed land properly, and conducted transactions in it. even then they were designated as sramanas. These Central Asian monks residing inside the monasteries (vihara, Sangharama), of course, could not attend the post-ceremony in the dress of house holder (grihastha coded in documents no. 489) the holy organization of the Buddhist church was called the Bhichu sangha (i.e., Bhiksu samghaj. All this has an important bearing on the great impact of the Hindu way of life in the Niya society in Chinese Turkestan during the first three centuries of the christen era.

BUDDHIST CULTURE IN KUCHA

Kucha was a part of Central Asia where Indian kings ruled in the ancient period. This country was situated in the north of the desert of Takla Makan, watered by river Tarim. It was an important region from the point of view of trade and commerce because one route passed through this region by which Chinese used to go in western countries for trade up to Kashagar. Sanskrit influence was brought to the countries of the north by Buddhism. But there is no evidence about the penetration of Buddhism in Kucha up to the present state of our knowledge. It can be accepted that it came not much later than the end of the 1st century A.D. In the 3rd century, we get a full picture of Buddhism so most probably it germinated in the soil of Kucha at least a century earlier. We have references to Buddhism in Kucha in the annals of the Tsin dynasty (a Chinese dynasty that flourished between 266 and 316 AD) which tells that in this period there were nearly one thousand Buddhist stupas and temples in Kuchas. Buddhist monks of Kucha used to visit China. it tells us about a member of the Kuchean royal family named Po-yen, who became a Buddhist monk and went to the Chinese capital in 256-260 in 258 He translated Shakas Buddhist texts into Chinese in the famous Buddhist temple of Po-ma- sse at Loyang.

Another Kuchean origin who went to China was Po-Sri Mitra. who visited China during the period 307- 312, and then on account of Political troubles moved to south China, where He translated Po-Yen, who was also a Kuchean (prince) went to Lang-Dhou in 273 was also a Buddhist scholar of repute. He knew several foreign languages but unfortunately, we have no translated text by him.

For Buddhist activities in Kucha, the 4th century A.D. is well known. This was the period when the Kucha was almost entirely a Buddhist city was commented in one of the Chinese texts. It further tells that even the place of the king looked like a Buddhist monastery with a standing image of Buddha carved in stone. There were several monasteries and few were established by the kings. Ta-Mu was a monastery where different numbers of monks lived i.e., in Poshan hill (che Ho li) 60, We-Su (Uch Turfan) 70, and so on.

The monks had to follow some principles. they had to change their residence at an internal of 3 months. after their ordination, If they had not passed at least five years, they were not allowed to stay in the new monastery of the king even for one night. This new monastery of the king had 90 monks. The same text refers to a young monk of this monastery named kiu kiu-kiu Skt. Mo-ki (i.e. Kumara) was a great scholar and studied Mahayana, a Buddhist text. It is a matter of strange that who was a disciple of Buddhasvamin who was the follower of aga-mas CHinayana), His disciple had become a follower of Mahayana. About the other establishment of Kucha, the texts tell that there was a monastery of Ali (Aranyaka) with 180 nuns. Besides it was the monasteries of Lium- Jo-Kan and Ali-po where 50 and 30 nuns lived respectively Buddhasvamin supervised monasteries and according to the country's rule, the nuns were not free to manage their affairs. The nuns who inhabited these monasteries were the daughters and the wives of the kings and nobles of the country as were to the east of the Pamirs (i.e., Tarimkasin) out of piety they came to these monasteries to live a religious life. They can not go out unless led by three senior nuns. They do not stay in the same monastery for more than three months. Thus, they observed very strict rules of discipline. They had to follow 500 rules.

It is most probable that Kumarajiva was the younger scholar of genius to whom the text had painted as kumara. about Buddhism in Kucha, the Biography of Kumarajiva also throws a good deal of light, which is preserved in Chinese sources, He was a son of Indian origin father named Kumarayana. His family was a family of ministers of this state. He embarrassed Buddhism and left for foreign countries after abdicating his rights in favor of his relatives He landed at Kucha after crossing, Pamirs, one of the difficult routes, where the king warmly welcomed and honored him as Rajguru. King had a daughter named Jiva. she fell in love with Kumarayana. Ultimately, the marriage took place and this couple gave birth to Kumarajiva. It is stated that soon after the birth of Kumarajiva, she became a nun, accepting Buddhism, and lived in a monastery called Tsio Li which was situated at a distance of 40 li to the north of Kucha, where she learned Indian languages.

Kumarajiva received full ordination in the king's Pamma-palace at the age of 20. He lived in the new monastery built by king Poshun. by the side of this monastery there was an old palace.

Kumarajiva discovered a manuscript of the Pancavimsati-Sahasrika Prajna-Parmita He explained the Mahayana sutras in the great monastery of Tsto-li. He also received a Kasmirian scholar Vimalaksa, with whom He studied Vinaya Pitaka. Now, taking permission from king Ho-Shan her mother (Jiva) comes to India to spend the rest of her life. It is stated that there were 10,000 monks in Kucha at that time. a Chinese expedition was sent against the Kucha in 392. They Invaded Kucha, and under the leadership of Len Chau after destroying the city they imprisoned a large number of Kuchean people, Kumarajiva was also among the prisoners. At first, He was ill- treated by the Lu-Kuang but soon when his merits were recognized Lu-Kuang treated him with respect and kept him at Leang-chow till 413. At the repeated request of the emperor, He was then sent to Chaangngan, the capital, where He worked till his death in 413. He translated there 98 texts and with him started a glorious Cpoch in the history of Chinese Buddhism.

Vimalaksha, who was staying in Kucha, joined Kumarijiva in China in 404 a few years later Dharma another Indian Buddhist Scholar came to Kucha and stayed there for a few years and them went to Tun-Huang was the place where sir Aurel Stein Discovered the cave painted with the influence of Ajanta, the well-Known Indian cave temple. He reached the Chinese capital in 424.

Among the personal friends of Kumarajiva the Kashmirian scholar, buddha Yasa, under whom Kumarijiva had studied in Kasagar, joined him there. He was also joined in China by another Kashmirian scholar, Buddha. In this manner, kumarijiva was the center of attraction. First in Kucha then in the capital of China for several years. So, He was responsible for introducing Mahayana in the countries of the Tarim basin, and also in China in an authoritative manner. He was one of the greatest proponents of this form of Buddhism and also of the Madhyamika philosophy. He introduced all these texts in China through his beautiful translations. his services were recognized by many Mahayana teachers of this period who were responsible for interpolating the name of Kucha in some of the canonical Mahayana texts. thus, in the Chinese translation of the Candragarbh sutra, which is part of the Mahasannilpata, in Connection with the various manifestations of Buddha, we are told that Kucha had 99 manifestations whereas aksu had 24.

According to this text, Kucha had her divine protectors.

Sravana was the protector of Kucha amongst the constellations.

So, Kucha received a special place of honor shown to the memory of Kumarajiva. another Indian scholar who came to Kucha towards the end of the 6th century A.D. was Dharma Gupta. Here he stayed for Two years in the king's monastery Mahayanist, the king of Kucha attached with dharmaGupta. before leaving for China, He Taught various sastras including the tarkashastra(logic). The Great Chinese traveler Huien-Tsang had written in the descriptions of his voyage about the Kucha that he passed through Kucha in 630. He further continues that these were 100 Buddhist monasteries in Kucha with more than 500 disciples at that time, followers of the Saravastivada school of Hinayana. They were a strict follower of the Buddhist customs of India, and read the original texts in Sanskrit. Among the especially famous monasteries, Huen Tsang mentions a few. about 40 li to the mentions north of the city there were two monasteries on the slope of the city where two monasteries on the slope of mountains which were called Chachu-li (the same as Tsio- Li of other accounts) the monastery contained a remarkably beautiful image of Buddha. The monks living there were pure, Truthful, and diligent in the discharge of their duties.

A SURVEY OF INDIAN RELIGION IN CENTRAL ASIA

It was some seventy years ago that Sir Aurel, Stein the great scholar, traveler, explorer, and eminent archaeologist during his archaeological explorations and excavations in Chinese Turkestan was able to unearth and bring to light from age-long oblivion a huge collection of Kharosthi documents about 782 in number. These records, written in Prakrit are available in the shape of small wooden tablets, leather pieces, Silk fragments, paper manuscripts, etc. pertaining to the everyday activity of the people in contemporary society as these documents are, they can throw a good deal of life on the social, religions and economic conditions of the region in early centuries of christen era.

The religion of Central Asia was of two types.

.1 Non-Buddhist and 2. Buddhist. Under non-Buddhist religion, it was the place where Indian gods and goddesses were worshipped in different forms along with their local names. They were worshipped in the same manner and customs as prevailed in ancient India. Sacrifices- sacrifices are a part of worshipping different Gods and Goddesses as well as evil spirits. It was done for the welfare of the family and society. fear and man born at a time (social contract theory of Hobbes, Locks, and Rosseau). We have many accounts of sacrifices from the Vedic period till in the 20th Century. Sometimes whenever kings of ancient India wanted to show themselves as the sole monarch of the world they performed those sacrifices (Ashvamedha). For example, Samudra Gupta when declined as the ruler of the world, performed those sacrifices the evidence is his coin types with legend (samadhi prakramah) and his Allahabad pillar inscription.

Even in the 20th century when we worship Goddess Kali a dirge, we us to give sacrifices. The same practice prevailed in Central Asia After a study of the pages of deciphered words recovered from Chinese Turkestan, recovered by Sir Stein we may conclude that the Central Asian people had a firm belief in the efficiency of sacrifices (skt. yajka). The truth of this statement is well corroborated by various phrases such as;

Yamana, kartavya, yanam, kitami etc. cows, sheeps and camels were sacrificied in Shansham kingdom, it is rather very surprising to note the offering of a cow for God bhatro (a savite God worshipped in Central Asia). The letters have been identified by D.C. Sircar with Bhadra (shiva) of Hindu pantheon. Once it so happened that a certain person saw in a dream the cow offered by him at the bridge (Indians also used to make offers besides bridge or sacred rivers i.e., Ganges) had not been accepted by the deity. not only that, that particular fellow saw the deity (in the dream) actually demanding a vitocow (a variety of cow like Indian kamadhenu) which according to him was to be scarified at the farm of a certain person called bkhara matgeya. since it was very essential to supply such an animal (i.e., vitocow) no. shackness was to be tolerated the matter. next time a "pursa sheep" (a kind of sheep) was to be sacrificed likewise. That is why the people in those Tseu tried to appear the gods and pacified their warm(anger). It should also be noted that the practice of sacrificing the animals was nothing now to the people in Central Asia. The Hunas1 used to offer horses for their Ist devatas (the god of family or race). They can mix wine with the blood of sacrificial animal and drank the mixture (thus prepared) in cups which were made of skulls2 of the slaughtered animals. The Samaritans (another Central Asia tribe) were more callous hearted. Herodotus records a funny custom prevailed among these barbarians who even went to length of sacrificing the human being (i.e., their relations who were on the versed death due to old age). Just after the sacrifice the flesh of the animals and human beings was boiled and used for feast in purposes.

----

1. A Central Asian tribe the Hunas in India by Thakur; (p I; in 1967.

2. As practiced by Aghoris in India.

death due to old age). Just after the sacrifice the flesh offering of flowers. Like in India the practice of offering flowers to the gods and goddess also prevailed in Central Asia. The evidence is the palaeographic some imprint of petals found near the scarified postage.

HINDU GODS

Now we will discuss the different Hindu Gods who were worshipped by the Central Asian people with different names Bhatro-already discussed in this chapter. Indra-next to bhatros (Bhadra or Shiva.) The God worshipped Central Asia people was Indra. Indra, according to Indian myths the god of Gods. The phrase: indram vivrdhi abhivarsata makhio udemta sa in No.511 has been interpreted in different ways by various scholars. according to Dr. Burrow, Makhi should be interpreted as lord of sacrifice (of skt makha=sacrifice) on the other Dr. Bailey quoating a stanza (of somewhat similar meaning) Harasadeva's ratnavate and priyadasika (i.e., urvim uddama janayatu visr. ijana vasaro vrstim istam)' tries to suggest that Indira was the God of rain and not of sacrifice. also Dr. Bailey refers to a Khotan "Dharni" where occurs toword Makhisavana corresponding to Tibetan Mahesvars. in addition, the Buddhist pantheon certain Hindu cults, Gods and goddess also came to be known in Central Asia quite early. as it is known Bhagawatism (the early form of vainais was firmly established in north western India during the male of the indo-greek kings one of the most important early Bhagawat records is the Garuda column of Besnagar which was erected in honour of Vashudeva, the God of Gods (Devadeva) by heliodorus, son of dion. heliodorous is described as a worship of Bhagawata and a resident to taksasita. He came to the cour of Indian king kasiputra Bhagabhadra during the fourteen years of his reign as an evoy from the Greek king Antralkidas, whoon numismatic grounds can be placed between (75 B.C. to 136 B.C. this shows that Bhagavatism became so popular during this time that even the foreigners were attracted by it. The spread of Krana cult outside India. for zenobs story of the Indian in Armenia it appears that the legend of Krana travelled outside India during 2nd cent B.C. two Indian chiefs, Zenab tells us, called orisan (kisane) and Demeter (temeter) fled west ward with their clan and found shelter with valarashak or valarasaces, the first Arsacid monarch of America (circa 149-127 B.C.) ped ginase and Demeter to death put their sons and decendents continued to live these they created two temples of their gods (ginase and denetes). but st. gregery invaded their temples and razed them to the ground. The Indians offered a stiff resistance, but were overpowered.

Demeter and gisana are names common to men and Gods.

Kennedy thinks that Demeter must be some compounds of mitra, perhaps Devamitra but about Demeter, He has no details, kisane as Zahab informs us, was represented with long hair. This worshipper also wore it long lesson suggested long ago, that Kisane might be identified with Krana. according to Kennedy, Demeter and Krana are probably forms of solar daticies.

If kisane is taken for Karna, then in my opinion, deva Mitra (Demeter) may stand for Baladeva, elder brother of Krishna The suffir mitra' is only indicative to his close solar and Vaisnavita association. The story of the flight to Gisane and Devamitra may be reminiscent of Krana and Balaram's flight to Dvarka from Mathura because of the pressure of their adversarie possibly this story went outside and got mixed up with a local legend in Armenia (J.R.A.S. Great Britain and Iceland 1904 p p.301 ff.).

THE CULT OF NARAYANA IN SOVIET CENTRAL ASIA.

In 1956, the Russian scholar A.N. Bernsam discovered in Tajikistan a fragment of Kharosthi inscriptions which has been translated by J. Harmata as Narayana, be victiorious, on Palaeograaphic grounds, the inscription can be attributed to the Second first century B.C. it is however, difficult to say that The 'Narayana mentioned here is the same as the Hindu Theology. if it is so, then it indicates the popularity of Narayana worship in Central Asia in the second half of first century B.C. It may be noted here that Narayana the Buddha is mentioned in the Khotan-saka documents in eastern Turkistan and Narayana the deva, occurs in the Buddhist Sogdiana documents (B.A. litinsky, Outline of history of Buddhism in Central Asia P.8, archaeology and culture of Central Asia in the Kusana period Dushanbe). On a tun-huans painting representing a thousand handed, thousand eyed Avalokitesvara, occurs an attendant figure, Narayana or Garuda (arther valley, a catalogue of paintings, recovered from tun hung P. 54. 1931). in all these contexts Narayana seems to occur in its Buddhist association, though it is quite possible that his Hindu feature were not completely unknown in Central Asia.

TRACES OF WORSHIP OF THE THREE CHIEFS' GODS OF HINDU PANTHEON

As to the popularity to the Visnu worship along with that of Siva and Surya, attention may be drawn to the Nicolo seal which was described first by Cunningham (1) according to him, the device consists of the four-armed pose of Vishnu with a devotee standing by his side in the respectful pose with folded hands the God has in his four hands a wheel, a mare, a ring like object and a globular thing. There is an illegible inscription by the side of the God. as to the devotee, Cunningham identified him as the Kushana king Ruviska because of the affinities of

1. Cunningham." the numismatic chronicle, PP. 126-127; Pl.X, fig. 2, London 1893.

Head dress and garment.

R. Ghirsman has however given the right interpretation of the seal by having deciphered the inscription correctly according to him, the inscription is in Tocharian script and contains in to Khrian language the names of Mihira, Vishnu and Siva. Further, he thinks that the devotee in question is not the Kushan King Huviska but some unknown hepthalite chief, About two or three hundred years later than Huviska in time, whatever it may be the use of Tocharian language and script on the seal shows beyond doubt that a composit cult of Siva, Visnu and Surya was popular with certain people of the Central Asia about five hundred A.D.

VAISHNAVA INFLUENCE ON BUDDHIST ART

Definite Vaisnavite influence is visible in a Buddha image with auspicious symbol from Balawaste in the Domoko region, On the southern Silk route of eastern Turkestan. This image attributable to about the 8th century, forms part of Stenn collection of wall paintings now preserved in national Museum New Delhi. The body and the arms of the figure are covered with symbol or devices including the Srivastasa, Diamonds, Mudra as churning rod, horse ucchaihsrava (indicative of the story of the churning of the ocean), the sun, the moon, vajra manuscripts Triangles a circle. taking the symbols into account, which have

----

(Banerjee. J. N.; the development of Hindu Iconography P.P. 124- 125 INDIA.)

no doubt, a mystic significance, it appears that the artist has tried to depict here the Viswarupa aspect of Buddha on the model of the Visvarupa of Krishna as narrated in the Gita. The cosmic aspect of Buddha has been emphasised also by the propounders of the Shingon creed which was very popular in Japan during the medieval period. according to Shigon belief, the body of Buddha comprises the whole cosmos, composed of the Shakas elements of earth, water, fire, air, ether, or vital energy and consciousness (M. Aneski, history of Japanese religion, pp 124-125). this Buddha has however life to do with the Shakyamuni Buddha and was called Mahavairocana.

CAIVISM IN CENTRAL ASIA

As to the popularity of Saivism in Central Asia, there is sample evidence. it is generally believed that Osama, the Well-known Buddhist philosopher of about 400 A.D. effected an amalgam of

Saivism and Buddhism. Rhys Davids writes in this connection. He (asariya) managed with great difficulty to re-council the two opposing myths by placing several Saiva Gods, both male and female in the inferior heavens of the Prevalent Buddhism as worship and supporters of Buddha and Avalokitesvara. He has made it possible for the half-converted and nude tribes to remain Buddhists while they brought offerings to their more congenial shrines and while their practical Religion had no relation at all to the truths or the noble Eightfold path. they busied themselves wholly with obtaining Magic power (siddhi) by means of magic phrases(Dharanis) and Magic charms (Rhys Davids, Buddhism p. 208 London 1877). Another reason for the amalgam of Buddhism and Saivism may be due to certain factors common to them. both Buddhism and Saivism were originally ascetic religions and both of them were Patronised largely by the merchant classes. whatever if may be the Saiva pantheon held the imagination of the Central Asia People over a wide area for a long time.

As is well known, Siva appears on certain coins of foreign Kings, Gondophares, Maues, and several others, the epithet "Deva" applied to Gondophares on coins is significant. The wood "Deva" is likely to mean here 'Siva' only and no other God. as an analogy we may draw attention to Hiuen-Tsang, 's references in his Si- Yu- Ki to Siva temple outside the gate of the city of Puskaravati, simply as a deva temple in the 7th century. An elaborate Siva Patheon is represented on the coins of the Kushana rulers (*2nd century). it is not only Siva but also his consort Uma and son Kartikeya-kumara that Frequently allegiance to Saivism as He is described as Mahesvara on some of his coins of vima and his successor.

Vima awed Personal allegiance to Saivism as He is described as Maheshvara on some of his coins. important Siva antiquity of the Gandhara region is the so-Called Tri murti image with siva as the Central figure. (c. 3rd.Century A.D.) from Akhum Dhevinear Charsadda. it is now preserved in the Peshawar

Museum. Regarding the spread of Saivism in west Asia, we may refer to the Greek author slobaus, who Quotes as passage from Bardavanes about the visit of an Indian To Synia at the time of antonious of emesa (218-22A.D.). This passage also contains striking reference to aradhnarisvaral1

THE MAHESVARA SIVA FROM CHINESE CENTRAL ASIA

The extension of Saivism of eastern Turkestan can be proved by certain finds in Dadan Uliq and neighboring sites of the Taklamakan desert. a very interesting representation of Siva Occurs on a painted wooden panel from Dandan-Uliq No. DVIL. 6. Its discoverer Sira. Stein describes it as follows- "We see a three-faced and four-armed divinity, seated cross-legged on a cushion, which is supported by two couchant bulls. The flesh of the divinity is shown dark blue throughout, except on two sides. heads of which on the right proper Coloured white bears an effeminate look while the other is dark blue with the expression of an ademon. The rich diadem of the Central head with its side ornament resembling a half-moon, the third eye on the fore head, the tiger skin forming the Dhotis, or loin cloth, and finally the bull represented as, Vahana all so many emblems, reflecting one's mind the Brahminic Shiva2

The popularity of Saivism seems to have extended to Sogdiana and eastern Turkestan during this period (i.e., the -8th century) this is evident from the discovery of a fragment of a wall-painting (depicting Siva) by professor A.M. Belenit sky in the course of his excavation at Piand ijikent, in 1962. Piandjikent is situated on the river Zervashan in Tadjikistan in the U.S.S.R. Shiva as represented in this fragment of painting, is provided with a circular halo and a decorted Yagnopavita. He stands in the Alidha attitude. as is the case in many Indian and Central Asian examples, He is clad in tiger skin. He is endowed with two eyes having a terrific look.

----

1. Fergusson, *History of Indian and Eastern Architecture; p.p 54.*

2. *Stein , A. Ancient Khotan Volume p.p. 279. Oxford.*

FORM OF SHIVA IN PAINTED PANELS

He has two arms shown akimbo. He is provided with various ornaments such as necklaces, bracelets, anklets, etc. A scarf with fluttering ends is shown round the forearms. Behind the left arm and left leg is shown shiva s familiar weapon, the trident. In the foreground, there is a cluster of plants recalling scanthus the plants are separated by a band of circular beads and below there is a lotus scroll. The deity is accompanied on either side by an attendant. One of the left bears a moustache and Ho has a dagger in a Scabbard hanging from the waist. He holds an incense burner with both hands the man on the right holds an incense burner with both hands. The man on the right holds a Chouri in his left hand. both the attendants have Sogdhian features and are clad in Sodhian dresses, and ornamental long coats with open collars. it may be interesting to note that thought Siva has been depicted in Indian tradition, the attendant figures have been depicted in Sogdhian style. this may be the skill of the artist who was accomplished in both traditions1.

WORSHIP OF SHIVA AND SAKTI

Unmistakable evidence of the presence of shiva-Sakti worship is provided by the Dandan-Uliq panel NO. D.X.8. The composition consists of a four-armed Trimurti form of Shiva and his Sakti who kneels on her right thigh. The God, with traces of the third eye, sits cross legged, cloth in tight fitting long sleeved white vest. Tiger skin pound the middle is shown with a point rising in from as in the case of the other Shiva figure from Dandan Uliq, mentioned with a point rising in the form as in the case of other Shiva figure from Dandan-Uliq mentioned above. This mode had been adopted perhaps to depict these figures as Urdhvamedhra or with erect phallus. as for comparison, mentioned may be made here of the Ithy phallic Shiva with Parvati by the side (Gupta period from

Koshan (This panel is now preserved in the Indian Museum, Calcutta) The main figure to be four armed, on one left arm is a massive armlet, while the other one Rasta on thigh and holds vajra. The lower right hand, as noted above, is thrown round the neck of Shakti, the objects on the other hand are long and wavy. The crown is of the usual Iranian type. The face to the left is fearful. and the third eye is visible. face to right is affected. The Shakti is dressed in a long Stona with tight sleeves to the wrist. with her right hand, she holds a cup to the deity she has well drawn eye-brows highly arched, and long eyes. She has a white complexion.

1 Arribus Asiae, volumexxxi Shiva icon from Plandjikent 1969.

TRIMURTI SHIVA

Shiva finds favour in Central Asia its existence of a shakti cult in eastern Turkestan during the 8th century A.D. is lent also by another Trimurti figure which is preserved in the National Museum, New Delhi. The deity sits full face with head lightly turned to the left. The other two heads project from either side from behind the ears. The centre face has a third eye in for head and a long thin moustache. The eyes are heavy-lidded and dreamy, on the head is shown a skull against the back top knot.

The deity has four arms, two upraised ones hold the sun to the left and moon to the right of the lower arms the right hand has a pomegranate held against the breast, and left-hand rests on the thigh grasping an un recognized attribute(vajra). The three heads (with the third eyes on the Central head), the skull on the headdress, and the attributes of the arms.

1   Stein   A : Ancient Khotan Volume l. p.p. 261 .pl. Lxll. Oxford.

Point to the Shaiva association of the deity.1

The other Hindu deities that occur in Central Asia art include Brahma, Indra, Ganesh, Kumara-Kartikeya, the Sun, and the Moon. and the Lokapalas etc. As adopted in the Central Asian Pantheon.

THE IMAGES OF BRAHMA AND INDRA

So far as Brahma is concerned, He has been noticed in the caves Of the Kucha area, and has already been referred to by coomarswamy.2 an interesting Figure of Indra occurs in a fragment of a wall painting from Balawasta, now preserved in the national museum, New Delhi.3 The figure is either kneeling or sitting with his legs crossed His body leans forward the hips with his head tilted back. The eyes are downcast and the hand folded and uplifted to neck-level The thumbs are strongly abducted, so that they are upright, While the fingers point horizontally. The head is covered with a close-fitting cap with a headband In a dark pink color, studded with white dots or pearls. The face is Indian with eyebrows to be met in certain Ajanta Figures(the figures wear many ornaments And Mukta Yajnopavita. it is endowed with a nimbus and on the Back of the right hand is out lined in black, an eye.

1.   *Andrews, F. Catalogue of Wall Painting from Ancient Shrines in Central Asia and System. Bal. 0200 pp 87. London.*

2.   *Coomarswami, History of Indian and Indonesian Art, London 1927, pp. 150 notes.*

3.   *Catalogue of Wall Paintings from Central Asia p.p. 13.*

The presence of the eye on the hand proves beyond doubt its identity with Indra1. Indra figure occurs also in some other paintings from Central Asia.

THE IMAGE OF GANESHA AND KUMARA

Ganesh, Kumara, the Sun, and the Moon have been noticed in the Tun Huang and a few other paintings of Central Asia. regarding Ganesh, attention may be drawn to his representation on a wooden panel from Endere. The God, with four arms, with an elephant head is shown seated. He is provided with a crown, and ornaments on his arms, wrists, and ankles. He wears tiger skin dhotis and tight Pyjamas. He has a rosary of dots and holds a bowl of fruits, A spearhead, a turnip, and an exe. The figure is attributable to the 7th and 8th century A.D. The details show that here is a representation of Ganesh being thoroughly Indian2. Dandan-Uliq has also yielded certain wooden panel sides depicting Ganesh. A fragment (dil. 16) represents him sitting on a die-pattern floor of a mat in two colors. He has a jeweled diamond on his head and has his trunk curled to his left.

Another fragment khadi (kh. 007) represents Ganesh seated on an open lotus. The right hand holds perhaps an Arikusa, and His left hand resting in the lap holds a round object. Ears are very large, and wing-like. All this wood attests to the popularity of Ganesha in the Khotan region. A fine figure of Ganesha occurs in cave 285 of Tun-Huang1. Andrews has noticed on a Bezeklik Wall Painting the representation of Kumar Kartikeya. Mahakala and Garuda carrying away nectar. In the upper register of the picture, Kartikeya is seated on a bird with one leg hanging down and the other tucked up in front. The hair, black, is shown in turts, the rest of the head is shaven. The figure has Shakas arms and in each hand is a symbol. two upraised

1 Banerjee, P. Indra from Balawaste (Indo Asian Culture) Volume xvii. no. 4. P.p. 14 ff.

2. Stein , A. Ancient Khotan Volume l. p.p. 431.-42 Oxford.

3. Ibid Volume l p.p. 292 ff.

hands carry in the right, red disc of the Sun, and in the left the left the white Moon. The next air the right hand is at breast, the left rests on hip, holding a long rod. The bird turns towards the rider. The clause is finely drawn.

THE MAHAKALA IMAGE

The second divinity (Mahakala) with a demon's head, is seated on a yak tail (Nandi) the mouth is open. hair cis flaming red. The upper hands hold elephants' skin of which the head and

1Gray, B. Buddhist cave painting in tun Huang p.p. 1-20London.1959

The trunk appears to the right. middle hand holds a flaming sword in the right and the left hand is missing. lower hands are both Missing, but the trident and vajra are visible1. In the lower register of this picture occurs again Kartikeya, and also the scene of carrying away Amrta by Garuda.

THE LOKAPALAS

The Lokapalas which were originally Hindu divinities, seem to be completely absorbed in the Buddhist Panthson of Central Asia. China and Japan. The four well-known Lokpalas are Dhrtarastra, Virudhak, Virupaksa and Vaisravana. they are considered in the Buddhist pantheon as Caturmaharajas, who guard the world against the asuras. each guards one side of Heaven, Dhrtastra, king of Gandharva and Pisacas, guards the East, Virudak, king of Kumbhandas, the south; Virupaksa, a King of Nagas, the west and Vaisranava or Kubera, king of Vaksas, the north.

These protectors of the four quarters are shown in Central Asian and far eastern as warrior kings with gorgeous Dresses and armour. they are sometimes accompanied by Yaksas or Demons as the case may be. Some of the earliest Lokpalas figures in Central Asia occur in the shrines of dan dan-Uliq and Rawak. The Lokpalas of Rawak shows a clear link with Gandhara's depiction. Wall-paintings and sculptures of Buddhist shrines near Kucha, Kara Shahr, and Turfan, and the Silk paintings of Tun Huang have Lokpalas representing plenty. The Lokpalas as stated above, were very popular also China and Japan.

1. *Andrews. P. catalog of wall paintings from Central Asian*

Shrines; p.p. 35-36. London.

2. *Stein , A. ancient Khotan; vol-l pp. 494 ff. fig. 67; Ll; pl. XIVLXXXV.*

BUDDHISM

BUDDHISM PLAYED IMPORTANT ROLE IN THE RELIGIOUS LIFE OF   CENTRAL ASIAN PEOPLE

The most important was the monastic life in Central Asia. The monastic life in India as well as in Central Asia underwent a great change in the course of seven Countries that intervened between the Tseu of Ashoka and those of Nalanda, Karle, and Nasik with corresponding changes in Central Asian monastic life. it appears that about the 3rd and 4th century A.D. The monks depended less on the collection of Aims and robes by begging and more on the food and robes procured from the income derived from the donations of lands, gardens, gold, silver, and other valuables. in the Karle cave inscription at the time of Nahapan his son-in-law Rsavadata made several gifts, one of which was the village of Valuraka to the Resident monks of Valuraka for the maintenance of monks of four Quarter during the rainy season retreat. in the Nasik cave Inscription of the time of Nahapan his son-in-law Rsavadata(Usavadata) dedicated a cave to the monks of the four quarters and made a permanent endowment of 3,000 Kahapanes (Karsapana)For the robes and other requisites of the monks residing in the cave during Varsavasa of this, sum 2,000 Kahapamas were to be converted in the guilts of Govardhana and one thousand Kshapanaa in the guilts of Chikhalapadra at different rates of an Interest. The interest of the farmer sum was to be utilized for the robes of 20 monks, who would enter into Varsavasa in that Cave, while the interest of the latter sum was for the requisites That might be needed by the monks. another cave inscription of Nasik of the same period records that a merchant Ramanaka, bestowed to the monks residing during the Varsavasa in that Cave. one hundred Karsapana to be sent at the rate of 12Karsapana for Civara of The monks (each) from July to September. from his inscription

It is quite evident that provisions of food and robes for monks Were made by the devotees with the income derived from cash

Documents from the produce of lands donated to the Saniha. Huen-Tsang writes about the monks of Nalanda That the king of the country remitted the revenue of about a Hundred villages for the maintenance of monks. we are told that Itsing (at the time of great king Harsha) stayed at Nalanda for a long time. Ho writes that the monastery of Nalanda was in Possession of more than two hundred villages bestowed by several Kings. there is a famous inscription of Devpala, who compiled at the request of Bal Putra deva, king of Suvarnadvip belonging to the Shailendra dynasty of java to construct a monastery and to grant five villages for the maximum maintenance of the bhikshus.

In the pre-Ashokan age, the Buddhist monks devoted Exclusively to religious, spiritual, and celestial practices without giving the least attention to economic activities. The fact that the monks lived as a corporate body in fixed abodes, usually, in the monasteries especially built for them cannot do away wholly with certain secular functions. The monasteries were no doubt provided by the lay devotes but These have to be planned and constructed according to the requirement of the monks. It is found in the Vinaya Pitaka that for the Proper management of the corporate body, several office bearers were selected and appointed. such appointments were made formally by the assembly of monks with 3 announcements and with the enormous consent of members present. The monks usually selected were of the best type and were supposed to be free from impulse. Hatred, delusion, and fear. it will be clear from the functions of the office bearer that monks had to give some attention to certain secular affairs, apart from their main religious and spiritual duties.

The name and brief Account of the office bearers as found in the Vinaya texts are as follows:

(1) Bhattuddesaka (distributer of food)

From the Chulavagga we learn that in Rajgriha there was once famine and it became extremely difficult for the people to maintain a supply of food to the communities of monks. This emergency necessitated the appointment of impartial distributors of food. when this matter was brought to the notice of the lord Buddha. Ho allowed gifts of food, specially meant for some monks. It was done by handing over sticks to the distributor of food. for a certain number of monks, whom a house- holder could afford to feed or by a general invitation of all monks on a particular day.

(2) Bhandarika (a store keeper):

The lay devotees offered robes and other requisites to the monks, as there was no fixed house, the articles were kept carefully at various spots, which were sometimes spoiled, and so it was decided that there should be a store house. There were many other officials to look after the activities of Monasteries. Niya documents furnish sufficient details about the Problems concerning the life of Buddhist monks and the scared Buddhist philosophy preached in Chinese Turkestan. People in These regions were fully acquainted with the rules of VINAYA. And, with the Buddhist creed and the related ceremonies. As regards the penetration of the Buddhist lore in Central Asia and the neighboring countries, the myths and legends Assign the 3rd century B.C. as the probable date of the Chinese Contact with Indian Buddhist missionaries.

It was in the year 2nd century B.C. that certain Buddhist texts Were said to have been presented for the first time by an Indo-Scythian ruler to the Chinese emperor. some centuries later, Dharmakala (an Indian scholar) reached China and translated the Pratimoksa (i.e., Vinaya texts) reached China and translated the pratimoksa (i.e., Vinaya texts) of the Mahasamhika school to Which he probably belonged. In the times of Fa-Hien Central Asian followers of lord buddha were seen studying the Indian books and conversing in that language.

VARIOUS TERMS FOR SUBLIME STAGES

Lord Buddha has been as (a) Buddha; (b) Gautama; (c) Saugata; (d) Tathagata; (e) Arahamata;(f) Konagamuni; (g) Prateyeka Buddha (h)Boddhisattva and (i)Jina.

(a) BUDDHA (of Buddha-Bhagavana No. 511) = Skt. Buddha, "the enlightened one". As regards the epithet Bhagava, it is identified as Sanskrit Bhagavata.

(b) GAUTAM; (of. lotamigrahiya vastra in No. 511)

(c) SAUGATA: one of the words used for Buddha.

(d) TATHAGATA: a stage to get Enlightment.

(e) ARAHAMATA: was applied to ascetic

In the general at the time of Buddha. (Of. Vedic arhamaha=Deserving). And Arahata has been described to possess a great many virtues. To the Buddhists it came to mean, who had attended the "Summum bonaim" of religious aspiration (i.e. nibaan). Gautam Buddha, before taking the vow of BODDHISSATTAVA, was in one of his incarnation, the Arahata called SUMEDHU. Chinese lo- Fan; Pali Arhata, are all designations of the perfect Arya, i.e. One who is not to be reborn. Arhataship employes possession of certain supernatural powers.

It was believed that the doctrine of the Buddha, If put in to practice, was sure to produce its subliming effect,

Niya document No. 511. i.e. all the creature that exists, on entering the path of TATHAGATA, make an end to the cycle of BIRTH and DEATH". That is why, prayers for abiding by the law of the blessed one were frequently made in No. 511.

The JINAS and the TATHAGATAS in No. 511 are stated to have been taking delight in the good of the beings. they were also endowed with the vision of the supreme truth. great reverence is shown for the JINAS, the TATHAGATAS, and the PRATAYEKA BUDDHA (NO.511). PARAMARTHA-DARSANA and BRAHMA-CHARIT were the highest ideals worth being cherished and lived for. References to the three sacred Pitakas have also been made in No. 511. The first Chinese addition to the TRIPITAKA S in manuscript form was collected in the year 518 A.D.

The document NO. 358 seems to refer to the Word NISAG in the scene of "bare necessities. of life but Dr. Burrow tries to identity it with PALI-NISSAYA meaning 'the fundamental requisites of life. Ho also thinks that the word NISAYA was imported from the Pali sources, but it is Too early to say anything with certainty.

BELIEF IN THE EFFICIENCY OF RELIGIOUS BATH

Document No. 511 enumerates the praises of "hot air baths", the health-giving virtues of which are celebrated with real enthusiasm. in the 58th and 100th AVADANAS, There the references to a particular kind of bath called the hot air bath". Thus, a Buddhist saint and his disciples Are invited by the head of a monastery to a meal and also to a "hot air bath' the morrow (the next day). The same Work furnishes details about these baths where as many as five hundred monks bathed in the hot and perfumed water.

1. Niya document no 511

2. Niya document no 399.

Mr. Speyer interprets the word JENTAK as a "sudatory room" and "JETAK SNATRA" as "a sweating room". The Carak Samhita refers to the word JETAK which means a bath room in which air was heated by the charcoal fire. in the Indian Buddhist lite Bathing rooms. we find references to the bath places and the Niya document1 attaches great importance to the gifts in matters about baths. the works connected with baths, it is an example of good action and the most excellent of the gifts. One, who is fortunate enough to avail the privilege of performing the Bath of GONOTTAMA following the works connected with heat, becomes 1 pure in Eyes, 2, bright in voice; 3. pure in limbs 4. Tender and good Complexion; 5. long-lived: 6. free from boils; Stephanotises itch: 7. pure and actions a sweat-smelling Body; 8. big eyes; 9. golden limbs and of a pleasing aspect etc. It is further prayed that "those who make Gifts on this point may enjoy the reward and let them be perfectly enlightened. Also, there are references to the bathing of monks in these baths. The Niya document also refers to the mighty touch of these baths when it runs thus;" may the monks, who bathe in the JAMADAKA baths, honor and love Their teachers, be pure in their current duties, with minds Free from hatred (or fault). In relation to these baths, one Who provides material for the removal of dirt or who provides a dry bath or denotes oil for rubbing be free from fault and impurity. it is now evident that donations of oil used to be made for the purposes and there was an arrangement for a dry bath.

1. Niya document No. 511; obverse

BUDDHIST MISSIONARIES

From the various sources, we came to know about the Indian Buddhist missionaries to Central Asia. Punyatrata and Dhara Mayasas have their names associated with the Chinese Translation of several important texts belonging to the SRAVASTIVADA school. Puniyatarata's name is given in Translation as "Fo-jo to Lo" and in transliteration as Kong-to-Ho. Ho went to Central Asia and China at the beginning of the 5th century and translated one work in 400 A.D. In collaboration with Kumarajiva. The Chinese biographers Tell us that Dharmayasas had come in contact with Punyatrata in Kasmir at the age of 14. The name is given in translation as "TAN MOYESHI AND transliteration as FAMINS. Ho left the country at the age of 24 and having traveled to various countries in Central Asia, reached China during the period 397-401

A.D. Ho translated 3 works into the Chinese. relation between Kucha and Kasmir was very close in this period.

Among those who had been to Kucha the name of Buddhayasas stands at foremost. Chinese biographers have left us a complete account of His activities in Central Asia. Ho completed his study at the age of 27 when Ho became a full-fledged monk. Ho then left Kashmir for foreign countries and first came to (Kashgar). The king of the country then Invited 300 Buddhist monks on a religious occasion. Yasas Was among them. his appearance and manners are so Striking that the king is very much impressed and invites him to live in the palace. At this time Kumarajiva came to Kashgar and met YASA. KUMARAJIVA spent some time there studying the sacred texts with Yasa and then returned to Kucha. KUCHA was then invaded by the Chinese army. The king of Kucha asked the king of Kashgar for help, but it was too late. Kumarajiva was taken into China as a prison. Yasa remained at Kashgar for ten years more and then went to Kucha. From Kucha, He wrote a letter to Kumarajiva expressing his desire to join him in the Chinese capital.

In this period, we hear of another Kashmirian scholar. Who was closely associated with Kumarajiva? This was VIMA LAKSA, who had first gone to Kucha and worked there with Kumarajiva. his name is given in translation as Pi-Mo-lo-cha and in transliteration as Wu-Ke-Yin. Ho traveled by Central Asian route and to China at the beginning of the 5th century A.D. Ho translated several Works himself and also explained the translations made by Kumarajiva.

Dharmitra was a Buddhist monk of Kashmir, who at first traveled to different places in Central Asia and then went to China in 424 A.D. Ho went to NAN KING, where Ho resided in Jetavahan (Che Huan Se) Vihar. Ho subsequently went to north China, where Ho died in 442 A.D. while in south Ho translated 12 texts Into Chinese.

Ajit Sena was a Buddhist scholar of northern India mentioned in Chinese sources as an achetasien. Ho Had gone up to Kucha which was then the seat of the Chinese Administration in Central Asia. Ho translated 3 works in the beginning of the 8th century.

AjitGupta was a Buddhist Scholar from Central India, reached the Chinese capital in 662 A.D. (in Chinese literature Ho has been painted as ati kiu to.) After traveling by the Central Asian route and translating between 653 and 654 A.D. Ho was assisted by two monks of MAHABODHI named Sarigha Nanda moksa and Kasyapa, who were in China.

Bodiruchi was a Buddhist teacher of Northern India and went to China by the Central Asian route Ho reached Loyang in 508 A.D. Ho was appointed head of the Buddhist community of 700 monks who knew Sanskrit. The famous monastery of YONG- NING-SSE was Built in 516 A.D. Bodhi Ruchi shifted to that place and worked there till 534 A.D. Ho translated 39 texts into Chinese. Subhakarsimha was the Buddhist monk of the SAKYA Family. in Chinese literature Ho is known by the name of Shen-Wu-Wei. Ho translated 5 works between 716 and 724 A.D. Upasunya was also a Buddhist monk of UJJAINI who Went to north China in 538- 39 A.D. Ho went to KHOTAN on an Imperial mission in 548 A.D. Ho translated all Shakas works. Prabhakar Mitra was born into a noble family in Central India and converted to Buddhism at an early age. Ho was educated at NALANDA and later became a teacher of great repute in that institution. Subsequently, Ho Left the country with several disciples to carry the Massages of LORD BUDDHA to a foreign land. Ho went to Central Asia. Ho translated three texts into the Chinese language.

But other parts of India were also Conscious of this great movement which was slow and Steady bringing the two great countries of Asia, India, and China through Central Asia. And China through Central Asia. from Central India.

Dharmasena was a Central Indian monk. his name is translated in Chinese as Tan-Mo-Chan. Ho was A follower of Mahayana Buddhism and at first went to Kasmir which was then a great seat of Buddhist learning. Ho then went to China by the Central Asian route. Ho was forced to remain at Kuet Sang which was then the Capital of an independent kingdom. Ho translated 25 texts Into Chinese.

Through various sources, we came to know that sending monks to preach Buddha law in different parts of India and foreign lands was in practice even at the time of Buddha. Warder, A.K.; Indian Buddhism.

4. LANGUAGE AND LITERATURE

BUDDHISM was the prevailing religion in this region as is shown by the discovery of which not only contains copious images and remains of hundreds of Buddhists shrines, stupas, and monasteries of design inspired by India, But, also by many Buddhist texts written in Sanskrit, Prakrit, or local language, largely in the Indian scripts, Brahmi and Kharosthi, Sanskrit dramas and texts on medicine, astronomy, and astrology, written in Brahmi have been discovered in Central Asia. Besides, hundreds of documents of administrative, commercial, legal, and miscellaneous kinds, drafted in Sanskrit, Prakrit, or Central Asian dialects, and written in Indian scripts as well as a complete alphabet of the Brahmi script have also been found in Central Asian sites, attesting a deep and abiding impact of Indian culture.

DISCOVERY OF SCRIPTS FROM CENTRAL ASIA

First of all, a British officer named Col. Bower, who was posted at Kucha, purchased from the local Turks an extensive Birch bark manuscript in 1890. this manuscript was dug out from the sands of Qumtura a site near Kucha. Later on, the same was sent to the Asiatic society of Bengal and was recognized by Dr. Hoernle to be a Sanskrit text of medical treaties written in north Indian script (Gupta) of the 4th century A.D.

Mr. Dutrull De Rhins second in the series, who was a French traveler, brought two birch Bark manuscripts from Khotan. it was a new version of Dhammapada in Prakrit. The script was Kharosthi of the 2nd century A.D. similar to that used in north-western India under Kusana. Later, its 2nd part was kept at Leningrad. These two discoveries diverted the attention of the archaeologists of the world. The government of India Disputed.

Sir Aurel Stein for the exploration of the Khotan region. German archaeologists under Grunwedel and Von Lacouq explored the northern part of eastern Turkestan in Turfan, Kucha, Karasahr, Kizil, and Bazaklik and recovered. A large number of art and literacy pieces. from 1906-1908 Stein explored Douoko, Niya, Loulan, and Miran along with the famous caves of Thousands of Buddhas. 2 in 1906 French sinologist Paul Pelliot collected archaeological remains from the caves of thousands of Buddhas. Russian also sent their mission under Berezovsky and Kazakoff.

1. Stein , A. "Ancient Khotan" Oxford.

2. Stein, A. ser-India Oxford.

The third time Stein explored Khotan, Niya Lou-Lan, Tun-Huang, Borkul, Guchen, Jimasa, Idikutshahri, and Aksu1. Japan sent its mission under Count Otani and Tachibana after 1904.

The literacy findings under Stein, Grunwedel, Von Lecoq, and Pelliot exhibit that Indian scripts were in use for nearly a millennium in different sites of Central Asia. during the first three centuries of the Christian era Kharosthi script was in use in the southern States, from Khotan up to Kroraina (Lou Lan) in the Lobnor Region Kharosthi as is well known was the common script of north-west India from the time of Ashoka up to the end of the Kushan period (third century A.D.). It was this script that was carried to the southern states of eastern Turkestan by Indian immigrants and was also adopted for official purposes. Kharosthi documents come mostly from the ancient sites Of Niya, Endre, and Kroraina, and are 782 In number. they are mostly in the form of wooden tablets, Leather pieces, Silk fragments, etc., and throw light on the Everyday life of the people. they contain a few Buddhist fragmentary texts but the character of the bulk of the collection Is generally profane and connected with the political and Economic life of the people. The manuscript of Dhammapada was discovered by Dutreuil du Rhins. and already referred to is in Kharosthi and belongs to this period. Kharosthi was supplanted by Brahmi in the 4th century A.D. and was adopted in the Khotan region as well as in Kucha and Karasahr in the north for literacy purposes. In The first stage it is the north Indian Gupta script that Was in use in the 4th century. it is used in the bower manuscripts, already mentioned, and the fragments of Buddhism Texts (especially Vinaya Pitaka) belonging to the weber Collection coming from the Kucha region. an isolated inscription containing the whole text of the Pyatitya Samutpada sutra discovered from Tunhung area is in also in this early Brahmi. Brahmi used in Kucha and Karasahr region during the Subsequent centuries is a local adaptation of the early Gupta whereas the earlier Gupta. has an upright ductus The later script is in a slanting style and is usually Known to the epigraphists as slanting Gupta. 'Slanting Gupta' did not come in use in the Khotan. Two types of modified Gupta scripts were used in this area-one is calligraphic and the other cursive. The Calligraphic style was used for literary purposes, especially for copying canonical texts of Buddhism. The cursive style was used in public and private documents as well as in secular literary works.

'Slanting Gupta' used in the north underwent some modifications to adapt itself to use for the local languages. in the Kuchean language and its allied dialect known as Tokhasian, Sanskrit sounds are somewhat attenuated and hence the corresponding Brahmi signs are under lined in the manuscripts. modified signs are also used for W. No such modifications were necessary for the calligraphic and cursive Gupta used in the Khotan area as two Khotan sounds foreign to Sanskrit viz. ys and rr or rr required no change in the signs. The documents reveal that use later the cultured people of the states of eastern Turkestan were familiar with two in-Dian languages, an Indian Prakrit and Sanskrit. The Prakrit Is the language of the Kharosthi documents from Niya, Endere, and Kroraina and of the Kharosthi Dhammapada from Khotan. This Prakrit is allied to the spoken language of north-west

India in which the inscriptions of the Kushan period are Written. it has some affinities with the literary Prakrit Described as (paisaci) by the Frakrit grammarians. as it was not a scared language of Buddhism it was not carried to Eastern Turkestan Buddhism monks but by actual immigrants from the north west to the Niya kerana region. The Language of the documents was the spoken language of the People till the end of the 4th century when the ancient Colonies disappeared. Sanskrit was introduced with Buddhism. Buddhism was introduced in the Saravastivada school of Hinayan Which had its stronghold in Kashmir and the north-west the scared literature of this school was written in Classical Sanskrit and this was the literature that was studied by the Buddhist scholars of the various states of Eastern Turkestan.

Mahayana Buddhism was introduced in the 4th century in Khotan. Kashgar and Kuchan. The literature Of Mahayana was also in Sanskrit medical and astronomical Treaties in Sanskrit were also studied by the local scholars. With the progress of Buddhism in the various states the necessity for translations of sacred texts into local Language was felt. But the local languages this raised to a literary status were also modeled after Sanskrit not only in their structure but also in the use of vocabulary. The technical terms, religious, philosophical, and scientific were largely adapted to the phonetic changes of the local languages.

SANSKRIT CANON

Until the decipherment of the Central Asian documents, the Pali canon was known to be the only authentic Sacred literature of Buddhism. there were however the Ancient Chinese translations of a complete Tripitaka but they were not based on Pali. The originals of these translations remained to be discovered. Central Asian finds came to throw an unexpected light on the problem and to establish for the first time that Hinayana Buddhism also possessed a complete Tripitaka which is now Lost. Central Asian fragments of the canonical texts belong to the Sanskrit Tripitaka. The Sanskrit tripittaka was the canon of the Saravastivada School and consisted of SutraPitaka, Vinaya Pitaka, and AbhidharmaPitaka. The SutraPitaka, was a collection of Aganas roughly corresponding to the Five Nikayas of the Pali TriPitaka, with the difference That there were four agamas in Sanskrit whereas Pali has Five Nikayas.

The four agamas called Dirgha, Madhyama, Samyukta, and Ekottara were translated into Chinese on different dates Between the 4th and 6th centuries. The Dirgha Agama was translated by Buddhayasas in 412-413, the Madhyamagama in397-398 by Gautama Sangghadeva; Samyukta Gama in 420-427 by Gunabhadra and Ekottaragm by Dharma Nandi in 384-385. All the translators hailed from Kashmir. This shows that the collections had been completed in Kashmir. before that 4th century, were widely studied there and were carried to Central Asia and China along with Saravastivada Buddhism Towards the end of the 4th century. The writing of the Central Asian manuscripts belongs to the same period. Of the SutraPitaka we now possess fragments of sutras of at least three agamas. they are the following:

Dirghama (1) Samgiti-sutra the fragment contains an enumeration of different dharmas into ten classes according to the number of items constituting such dharmas. There is a Samgitisuttanta in Pali Digha-Nikaya but the Sanskrit text agrees more with the Samgiti-Sutra of the Dirghama in Chinese translation.

(2) Ata-Natiya-Sutra is very different from the Pali at-anatiyasuttamta but a similar text under the title Mahasa-Maya-Utra is found in Chinese Dirghama. The Atanatiya-Sutra may be a later elaboration of this text. Madhyamagama-(1) Upalm-sutra which is different from the corresponding Pali text (Majjhima56) but agrees with the Chinese translation (madhyamagama133). (2) Suka-Sutra a text dealing with the doctrine of karma and retribution the Pali text (Majjhima 135) has a different title-culla Kammavubhanga which is more elaborate. The fragment agrees with the corresponding text in Chinese madhyamagama (text No. 170). The text was very popular in Central Asia and China as shown by its translation in the language of Kucha and four separate Chinese translations which still exist.

Samyukta gama-(1) Pravarana- sutra- the fragment of the Sanskrit text agrees with the Chinese translations of Gunavarman. there are two other separate Chinese translations of the text, one by Dharma Ksema made in 266-317 A.D. and the other by Fa-Hien

(Dharmabhadra) in the 10th century. The text has some general agreement with Pali Vangisa-Thera-Samyutta of the Samyutta-Nikaya. (2) Candropama Sutra-The fragment has a general aggrement with the Pali Samyutta (third sutta of the Kassapa section) but agree more closely with the Chinese translation. (3) Sakti-Sutra corresponds to Pali Satti-Sutta of the Opamma section of Samyutta-Nikaya. There is a later Chinese translation of the text. (4) Nidana Sutra dealing with the chain of causation and with the means of its destructions corresponding with Pali Nidana-Sarthyutta-Nikaya (xiii, 15) also found in the Samyutta Chinese translation of the Samyutagama. there are also independent Chinese translations of the text. (5) Kokanada Sutra (=Chinese translation of the Samyuktta 34, Pali Anguttara 196-198) (6) Anathapinada-Sutra (Samyukta 34, Pali Ang. v 185-189). (7) Dir-Ghanakha-sutra (Samyukta 34-35 Pali Majjhima 487-501) (8) sara-Bha-sutra (Samyukta 35, Pali ang. 185-188) (9) parivrajaka-Sthavira-sutra (Samyukta 35), (10) brahmana-satyamsutra (Samyukta 35). The viaya of the Sarvzimstivada school is well representedly the fragment of texts coming from the northern part ofEastern Turkestan. like other sections of the canonical literature of the school the Vinaya Pitaka was written in Sanskrit. The pratimokas-sutra belonging Saravastivada Vinaya was discovered by the French mission In the Ruins of duldur. aour at Kucha. The text contains all the sections such as Nidana. Parajika. Sanghadisesa, etc. The Pali. Patimokkha corresponds in major part with the text. its Agrees literally with the Chinese translation made by Kumarajiva in 404A.D. Bhiksunipratimoksa of the school is presented by fragments discovered in the Kucha Region by both French and German missions. Besides a very important text entitles Maha Parinirvana-Sutra belonging to the Mula Saravastivada . Vidaya which also were wrote in Sanskrit has been restored from a number of fragments discovered by the German mission from the ruins of Sorcuq near Turfan and of Tums Huq near Moral-Bashi. Parallel texts were also discovered from the ruins of Kizil near Kucha. Mula Saravastivada School was development from the Sarvastida and flourished in Kashmir.

it possessed an extensive Vinaya Pitaka in Sanskrit but it was known for many years only from the Chinese and Tibetan translations and several fragments Contained in the Nepalese called Divayadana. The considered position of the original texts has now been restored from manuscripts discovered in a ruined Monastery in Gligit by Sir Aurel Stein. The Mahapariniryana Sutra from eastern Turkestan belongs to this Vinaya collection and agrees with the Mahavagga of the Pali Vinaya Pitaka The Abhidharma Pitaka of the Saravastivada school was also known and studied in Central Asia. this Pitaka consists of seven texts of seven texts which are preserved in Chinese translations but a fragment of the original Sanskrit text of the Sangi Tibaraya has been discovered in the caves of Bamiyan in Afghanistan. The script is "Slanting Gupta" which was in use in the northern part of eastern Turkestan Fragment of a new sutra that belongs to the Sutra Pitaka of Hinayana but has not strictly included in Any of the agamas has also been identified as Dasabalsasutna Mahavadanassuta, saptabuddhaka etc. The Dasabalasutna was a very popular text. It agrees partially with Pali Dasakanipata of the Anguttara-Nikaya and the Dasaka Section of Chinese translations of ekkottaragama. there's also a separate chinse translation which was made in Kucha towards the end of the 8th century by the ChineseEnvoy wukoyong in collaboration with a kuchen monk

Named W-Ti-Ti-Siyyu. Mahayana canon was also studied in Central Asia. Fragments of a few important texts amply prove this. There are fragments of: (1) Vajra-Chedika belonging to the prajnaparamita class, (2) Ratna-Rasi-Sutra of the Ratnakuta class, (3) Ratnadhvaja, Candra-Garbha and Candrapala Sutra of the Mahasannipata class, And (4) Mahaparinirvana-Sutras of the Nirvana class. we have besides fragments of the two other major texts Of Mahayana, viz. -this Saddharmapundarika-Sutra and suvarna Prabhasottama-sutra. texts on dharanis or magical formulae Belonging to later Mahayana; have also been found eg. Anantamukha-Dharni, Suramgamasamadhi and Sitata-Pitatra-Dharni.

TWO IMPORTANT TEXTS:

DHAMMAPADAAND UDANYARGA were two important recovered from Central Asia, being in Pali and SANSKRIT languages, respectively. Dhammapada is a unique text consisting of very old verses many of which are found in different parts of the canon. The verses were arranged in sections and put in the form of a present compilation later by an author whose name is lost. Besides the PALI Dhammapada, we are now in possession of two other similar Collections from amongst the Central Asian finds. One of them is the Dhammapada in Prakrit and the other is the Udanavarga in Sanskrit.

Dhammapada which was recovered from Khotan of the Prakrit language was written in the Kharosthi script of the 3rd Century. The language is different from Pali and is a middle Indo-Aryan which is akin to the dialect spoken in North-western India in the Kushana period. of the period immediately preceding. The text is fragmentary and some verses from the sections entitled Apramad, Cita, Pusa, Sahasa, Panita, Pala Jara and Sudha have come down to us. a clear idea of the difference in language may be formed from the following verses.

PRAKRIT

अप्रभदु अगुत चद प्रभदु मुचुनो पद !

अपरभात न भियन्ती य प्रभत यदा मुतु !

अप्पभेदो आगतपदम पदमो गुचुनो पदम् !

अपभाता न भियन्ती ये प्रभानता यचा मता !

अपरभादो प्रभादो मृतगुण: पदम्!

अपरभानता न भ्रियन्ते ये प्रबंता: सदा मृता:!

The Pali Dhammapada belonged to the THERAVADA school. So, the Prakrit Dhammapada belongs to a school which wrote in Prakrit. Stein, Grunwedel and Pelliot mission brought from Central Asia fragments of scripts of Sanskrit text called UDANVARGA.

The Grunwedel and Pelliot manuscripts are almost complete. fragments from Stein collection was published by La Valle Roussia. The complete section of YUGAVARGA was edited from three manuscripts of the German collection by paschal under the title (Turfan recension of Dhammapada. Leivi edited the first section, Apramadavarga was from the French (2).

The whole Text of Pelliot's manuscript was later edited and published by Dr N. P. Chakravarti. The text of the Udanavarna, written in Sanskrit is a collection Akin to the Dhammapada, in some places more extensive. The Collection is attributed to Dharmatrata, a famous teacher of the Saravastivada school who was contemporaneous with Kanishka, and level in the first century. The Tibetan translation under the name Udanavarga had been rendered into English by Rockhill. Dhammpada texts in their various recensions were very popular in Central Asia and China. besides the two local texts Already mentioned translations in local languages had also been made and were widely read. there are four Separate Chinese translations, based on four different Recensions of the text, three of which had been carried from Central Asia to China. they are (1) Fa-Kiu-King- Dharmapadassutra translated in 224 A.D. (11) Fa-K'iu-P'iyu king-Dharmapadada-Avadana sutra translated between 290 and 306 A.D.;(111) chu Yao king translated in 398-399 A.D. The last-named text is the translation of the Udanavarga. The first two translations were probably based on a text similar to that of the Prakrit Dhammapada.

Political works- Asvaghosa & Matrceta Remains of the works of the two great Buddhist poets Asva Ghosa and Matrceta were discovered among the Central Asia finds. fragments of the works of Asvaghosa were brought by the German mission from the Turfan region. Asvaghosa Is a well-known scholar and was a contemporary of King Kanioshka and a philosopher, poet, and dramatist of the first order. two of His poetical works, Buddhacarita, and Saundarananda are Known as original, and a third, the Sutralamkara is preserved In the Chinese translation of Kumarajiva. besides a philosophical Work entitled Sradhotpada-Sastra has also been Preserved in Chinese translation which is widely studied in China and Japan. Central Asian remains throw more light on his other works. A fragment of the Buddhacarita brought from the Turfan region Shows that the text was studied by the Buddhist monks of Central Asia. a drama entitled Sariputra-prakarana discovered in the same region and not known from other sources is ascribed to Asvaghosa. only portions of the original work have been Found. but they clearly show that it was a remarkable work. It is the oldest Indian drama known to us and presupposes A great development in dramatic art. The work is in Sanskrit but there are dialogues, in Prakrits which are older than the dramatic used in classical Sanskrit dramas. Another work of controversial authorship was also discovered by the German mission in the Turfan region. it is a poetical Work in Sanskrit that agrees with the sutrlamkara of Asvaghosa as known from the Chinese translation

of the work by Kumarajiva. but the colophons of the Turfan manuscript ascribe the work to Kumaralata. The colophon runs thus: Iti drya Kumaralatayam Kalpanam and Drastantapanktyam. We have sometimes the word Kalpanamanditikayam instead of Kalpanalamkrtayam. Kumaralata, in one context is described as a Bhikkhu of Takashia(Taxila). Professor Ludres who deciphered the manuscript, edited, and published it was of the opinion that the name of the work Was Kalpanamanditika and that is author was Kumaralata. The Chinese tradition ascribed the work to Asvaghosa through mistake. Kumaralata was of course a well-known Buddhist scholar of Taxila. his name is transcribed in Chinese as Ku-Mo-Lo-Lo-To and translated as tong shou "boy-received". The Tibetan Tradition says that Ho belonged to the Sautranika school.

The Buddhist tradition further records that Ho was the Sun shining in the north while Asvaghosa illuminated the East, Nagarjuna the west and Aryadeva the south" Kumarlatas fame was so great that Ho was taken by force to the country of Kie-pan to i.e., Taskurghan in the Pamir. Ho is said to Have composed many shastras but none has come down to us Either in original or in translation. The Turfan manuscript However attributes the present work to him. Kumaralata is described in Chinese tradition as a "master of comparison" (Darstanika) which was a branch of the Sautrantika school. The principal work of Kumarlata is mentioned in The Chinese text as Yu Man Lun- Drstanta-Mala (Pankti)-shastra on these grounds Levi has expressed the opinion that the name of the Turfan text was distant-Pankti (as found in the colophon) and that Kalpanamanditika is an adjective to it. The Turfan text is considered by Levi to be a new addition of the Sutralamakara of Asvaghosa expanded by the addition of moral lessons and a Poloues in the form of examples (Drstanta) according to the practice of the Darstantika school. The Turfan text therefore Represents partially the Sutralamkara of Asvaghosa. The hymns of Marcela: the fragments of the poems of another Poet of great fame have been brought to light both in Sanskrit original and Tokharian translation. The poet was Matrceta who is well known from Tibetan and Chinese translations a full account of the poet and his works is given by Yi-Tsing (Takakusu-Buddhist practices in India pp. 156 ff.) "In India" Ho says," numerous hymns of the praises to be Sung at worship have been most carefully handed down, for Every talented man of letters has praised in verse whatsoever persons Ho denied most worthy of worship. such a man was the venerable Matrcetas, who by his great literary talent and virtues, excelled all learned men of his age.

The Following story is told of him: while the Buddha was living, Ho was once, while instructing his followers wandering in A wood among the people. A Nightingale in the wood, seeing the Buddha, majestic as a gold mountain, adorned by his perfect Signs, began to utter its melodious notes, as if it Sang in praise of him the Buddha, looking back to his Disciples, said:' the bird transported with joy at sight of me, unconsciously utters its melodious notes. on account of his good deed, after my departure (nirvana) this bird shall be born in human form, and named Matrceta, and Ho shall praise my virtue with true appreciation.

previously as a Follower of another religion, when born as a man, Matrceta had been an ascetic and had worshipped Mahesvaradeva. when a worshipper of this deity, Ho had composed hymns in his praise. but on becoming acquainted with the fact that his birth had been fore told, Ho became a convert to Buddhism, robed in color and free from worldly cares. Ho mostly engaged himself in praising and glorifying the Buddha, repented his past Sins, and was desirous henceforward of Buddha's good example Regretting that Ho could not see the great teacher himself but his image only. in fulfillment of the above prediction, Ho wrote hymns in praise of the buddha's virtues to the greatest extent of his literary powers. "Ho composed first a hymn consisting of four hundred a S'lokas, and afterward another of one hundred and fifty. Ho treats Generally of the Shakas Paramitas., and expounds all the excellent Qualities of the Buddha, the world honored one, these charming Compositions are equal in beauty to the heavenly flowers, And the high principles which they contain rival in dignity The lofty peaks of a mountain. Consequently, in India all Who compose hymns imitate his style, considering him the father of literature. even men like the Bodhisattvas Asanga and Vasubandhu admired him greatly. throughout India, everyone who becomes a monk is taught Matrceta's two hymns as soon as Ho can recite the five and ten precepts. 'Of the two works of Matrceta, Yi-Tsing while in Nalanda Translated one in 150 verses into Chinese. it was revised by Him later on in China (708). The Chinese catalogues render the Title as Sardhasataka-Buddhaprasamsagatha but the original Sanskrit title is now as Satpancasatika Stotra. As the Colopbion of the Tibetan translation of the Satpanca-Satika Stotra attributes the work to Asvaghosa and as taranath Also takes him to be identical with Asvaghosa. Matrceta has been considered to be another name for Asvaghosa. in a way Matrceta was also a contemporary of Kanishka, and if not Identical with Asvaghosa, was just his elder contemporary and lived in the first century A.D. The tradition that Yi-Ting records about teaching the hymns of Matrceta to all monks is probably very old. that is the reason for why the hymns seem to have been very popular in Central Asia too. manuscript of the Sanskrit original of the Satpancasatika-Stotra have been brought from various sites in Central Asia such as Jigdalik-Bai, Tunhuang and Khotan.

Tokharian translations of the text have also been brought by the German expedition from Turfan. The various fragments of the Sanskrit manuscript have brought to light the following verses: 23-38, 48-74, 117-181, and 146-150 (Hoernle pp. 58ff.). fragments of verses 147-150 were also discovered in a leaf in the Pelliot collection (Levi, j. As. Isbu. 450). two verses may be quoted here as examples of the position of Matrceta....

"From the mingled, only the faultless essence was taken into the mind at once, the well said: but the ill-said like Poison was avoided.

By the shower of the world of jewels, purchasing With Life what was well-said, heroism was shown for the Shakas of bodhi in a variety of births." Fragments of other work of matrecta, the catuh' saiaka-stotra also have been discovered from Central Asia. There is no Chinese translation of the text but the Tibetan translation give the name of work as Var nanarha- Var nanastotra. Fragments of Sanskrit manuscript were discovered from Khotan (near Karasahr) and Udanqulik (nearby). only thirty-two verses have been discovered from the fragments and it appears from them that the text was divided into 12 chapters, we have all Verses of chap. 1, 9 of chap.VI, 2 of chap. vii and 10 of chap. XII.

The colophon of the chapters gives the full title of the work as Var nanarha-Varne Buddhastotre catuhsatakam, the literary value of the verses is as great as that of the other work:

(7) Ah, the misery of samsara Ah, the peace of nirvana though

Ho is a lord, Ho went there (i.e., into samsara), having a Soul of pity like thine. (8) future fears were certainly told; guidance was certainly Prompted: mundane existence of four kinds was certainly made to attend fearlessness.

SAVSKRAH MEDICAL TEXTS

Buddhist missionaries carried to Central Asia not only Indian religions and literature but also scientific knowledge. We have indirect evidence of the use of Indian astronomy and Mathematics, but no manuscripts of astronomical; and mathematical texts have so far been discovered. The literary remains brought from the ancient sites however contain a large number of fragments of Sanskrit medical texts which were used in Central Asia from the 4th to about 8th century A.D.

Col. Bower discovered three different medical texts from an old stupa near Kucha they are usually known as bower manuscripts one of these texts deals with Karaghalika, its origin, and use. The other says that Karaghalika can oure many diseases and can extend life up to 100 years. The texts also deal with Digestion, an elixir for a life of 1000 years, correct Mixing of ingredients, other medicines, lotion, and ointment for Eyes, etc. The second text contains 14 medical formulae for external and internal use. The third text which is the largest Portion of the collection is called Nantika, "cream" and contains an abstract of the earlier medical literature. it deals with the preparations of powder, decoctions, and oils and also with injections, elixirs, aphrodisiacs, nursing of children, etc. The earlier literature quoted in the text includes Agnivesh. Bheda, harita, jatukarna, ksarapani parasara and susruta. Besides the Sanskrit original medical texts, there is other Evidence to show that Indian medical literature was widely used in Central Asia. we know from translations of Indian texts into Kuchean and Khotan languages that the knowledge of Indian medicine was very wide spread. Indian medicine was very wide spread. these translations bear out the local doctors who did not know Sanskrit were making use of the Indian system.

LOCAL TRANSLATION

We have already spoken about the Kuchien and Tokharian languages before (ante pp. 68 ff. and p. 28 ff.) the language of Kucha Which was known to the Uigur Turks under the name Kusana was spoken in the earlier region from Aksu (ancient bharuka) to the Turfan (ancient agnidesa). Literary remains in this language have been discovered from different parts of this region mainly by the French Archaeological mission. A few fragments also belong to the stein collection and a few others were found also among the German and Russian collections. The fragments of kuchen texts of the site and Russian collections were studied and published along with the French collection by Sylvain Levi and later byJean filliozat (texts koutcheens fragments de texts koutcheens De medicineet de magie), Kuchean texts of the German collection were never published.

The fragments of texts in the other dialect which has been called tokharian were discovered by the German missions in Karasabr and Turfan region. The spoken language of the area However, We have seen was Kuchean. The mural inscriptions in the Buddhist caves in this area, are also written in Kuchean Tokharian literature in all likelihood was developed in some other area probably in Tokharistan and the texts had been Brought to this region during the Uigur period. The German Collection of 417 fragments were edited by sieg and siegling and published with plates in a volume entitled tocharische sprach-rest aong the fragments and the rest from the sites of the Bajaklik, Murtuq. Sangim and Idikutshahri at Turfan. Kuchean and Tokharian fragments are all translations of Sanskrit Buddhist texts and contain some bilingual pieces with original Sanskrit by the side of translations these bilingual pieces were of great help in the interpretations of the language. The Kuchean fragments have been fully studied and identified. We have fragments of the Kuchean translations of Saravastivada -Vinaya such as Pratimoksa, Pryascittika, and Prabidesa Niya. These canonical rules of monastic disciplines were of constant use to the Buddhist communities in Central Asia and required Translations in local language so that monks not well versed In Sanskrit could understand their implications. The bilingual Texts must also have been used as handbooks for teaching Sanskrit to the local Buddhists.

we have besides Kuchean Translations of Udana Varga, Udanastotra and Udanalamkara which were very popular with the Buddhists. there are also Fragments of kuchen translations of a very extensive Sanskrit work entitled Kumar Vibhanga, a text on the retribution of Acts (karma) which was used by the Buddhist priests as a handy text illustrative of the doctrine of transmigration. Kuchean translations of medical and tantric texts have also been studied, identified, and published. We have already mentioned the translations of a medical text entitled Yagasataka. It is a work in about one hundred verses attributed sometimes to Nagarjuna and sometimes to Vararuch, the original Sanskrit text is known through Nepalese and other manuscripts and also through a Tibetan translation. The Yogasataka was an excellent abridgment of standard Sanskrit medical texts and a convenient handbook used by medical practitioners in India and abroad. we have several fragments of the Kuchean Translation of medical texts from Pelliot, Stein, and Weber collections. These have not been identified on account of their fragment character but comparison with such medical texts as Charaka and Sustra shows that they were based on standard Indian texts. Sanskrit names of drugs are not translated but transliterated with phonetic changes necessary for their adoption in local languages examples rirak (haritakt), kurkam(kurkuma), akanu(aguru), Asvakanta (asvagandha), apamarka (apaunarga), etc. Fragments of translations of Buddhist texts in the other dialect called. Tokharian, although published has not been closely studied. they contain bilingual texts and have among them such popular texts as the Udanavarga. Ancient Khotan known through the translations of Buddhist texts was at first described as 'North-Aryan', and subsequently as Saka language. although the name 'North-Aryan has been totally described some scholars persist in retaining the name Saka. whether it was exclusively a language Spoken by the Shakas still remains to be determined. as the Khotan presented by the translations is found for the first time in a late form in documents of the 7th - 8th Centuries when Shakas were practically forgotten, it is safer to describe the language is we have done before as eastern

Tokharian dialect.

Translations belong to a late period Wghen Hinayan Cally disappeared from the Khotan region And Mahayana had become the predominant religion. The translations therefore are mostly of Mahayana texts. we have so far fragments of the translations of the Suvarnaprabhasa-sutra, Vajracbhedika, Aparinitavus-Sutra, Bhadracaryadesana, Jataka-Stave, and Maineeya-Samiti-Nataka. Khotan translations of two Indian medical texts also have been found. These are the Siddhasara and Jivakapustaka. The Siodhasara is attributed to one Ravi Gupta.

The Khotan rendering was based on the Tibetan translation. The fragment Contains portions of the following chapters: Tantra, Dravya, Arsa, Bhagandara, Nanouroga, Nubrakrccha, Udavarta, Netrapia, etc. In original of the other text, the Jivakapustaka has not been traced but the interlinear Sanskrit verses show that it was Sanskrit. Sogdian language, we have seen (antep.38) was spoken not only in ancient Sogdian but also in other parts of eastern Turkestan where colonies of Sogdian merchants had been established. It might have been as suggested by Pelliot, a sort of lingua France in Central Asia. It was used by Manichaean Priests in the Uigur period in the 9th and 10th centuries A.D. But earlier the Buddhist priests also used it. A few Sogdian translations of Buddhist texts have been discovered. These are the dirghanakhasutra, Vessantara Jataka, Vimalkriti, Mirdesa, Dhyanasutra, Dhuta-Sutra, Nilakantha-dharni and Padmacintamani - Dharni-Sutra. With the establishment of the Uigur empire with its capital in the Turfan region in the 9th century Buddhism found yet another Patron in the tusks. they assimilated the entire Buddhist Culture prevalent in Central Asia from the Oxus Valley up to Karasahr, with its literature, religion, and art. Tokharian Buddhist texts were translated into Turkish, we have thus translations of Maitryasamiti-Nataka, Suvarnaprabhasa- Sutra, jatakas, the sutra of Kalyanamkara and Papamkara, etc. although We have a few Turkish documents in Brahmi, knowledge of Sanskrit was almost obsolete. a new epoch of Buddhism had started and India did not play any direct part in its transmission.

NEW ASPECTS

Buddhist literature in the course of its migration from India to China assumed new aspects in Central Asia. The famous Monasteries of Central Asia became active centers not only for the preservation and propagation of the canon but also for its reconstitution. In the course of their literary activities, conscious efforts were made by the monks to naturalize the canon by introducing such elements as would make it Ser-Indian literature as well. Pseudo-canonical Mahayana literature was also created in different parts of the Country. Chinese evidence dating from the middle of the sixth century tells us that the country of Cokkuka near Khotan (Antep. 48) was a great center of Mahayana Buddhism. The king of the was also devoted to this faith. when monks from other countries Came to cokkuka they were first to submit to an examination. If they were found to be followers of Hinayana they were sent back. if they were found to be Mahayanist they were invited to stay. in the palace of the king, there were copies of the great sutras. Mahaprajanaparamita, Mahasannipata, and Avatamsaka, the king himself were their custodian and kept The keys of the chamber where they were stored. He opened The doors every time they were to be taken out for reading and then kept them safely back. other sutras were jealously Guaraised in a precipitous mountain in the neighborhood of Cokkuka. The following sutras, all Mahayana were kept there: Mahasannipata, avatamsaka, vaipulya, ratnakuta, lankavatara, Sariputra-Dharni, Mahaprajnaparamita, Astasahasrika -Prajnaparamita, and mahemegha. The canonical sutras mentioned above were no doubt of Indian origin but an analysis of some of them from their ancient Chinese translations clearly shows that they were naturalized in India.

The Suryagarbha and the can dragarbha are two important sutras of the Mahasannipata collection. They are preserved in a Chinese translation of about the middle of the sixth century by Narendryasas; the Sanskrit original of the texts is now lost. The Suryagarbha-sutras in one of its sections mentions Buddhists' Holy places. in this list, we have the holy places in India. cinasthana(chima), Khasa(kashgar,) and Gomasalagandharacalitya on the Gosrnga mountain of Khotan. was according to the text one of the hilliest places visited by myriads of Buddhist devotees, we already know that Gomsalagandha was a historical place in Khotan (ante p. 53) The can Dragarbha-Sutra contains two lists of places hallowed by Buddha. In the first list, we have mentioned 53 kingdoms among which the following belong to the ser-Indian regions: Askoka, darada, khasa, cokkuka, and Sha-lei (Kashgar). Khotan, Kucha, Bharuka, Hecyuka, Yi Ni (Agnidega). Shan-Shan (Kroraina) and Cinasthana. In the second list, we have an enumeration of the number of incarnations of Buddha in various countries. In countries outside India, silica (Sogdiana) had 28, Posse (Persa) 20, Khasa28, Cokkuka20, Khotan180, Kucha99, Bharuka24, Hecyuka18, yini(agni) 80m Shan-Shan (Kroraina)28 and Chinese 255. judging by the number of incarnations Khotan, Kucha, and China are given places of the greatest ~~honour In~~honor in the Buddhist world. The Chinese sources contain the story of the tragic death of An Indian Buddhist scholar Dharmaksena during his journey to Khotan in order to get complete Caonical texts. Dharmaksena belonged to Central India and was a follower of Mahayana. Ho had found in his own country only ten chapters of the ~~fnous~~famous Mahayana text the Maha Parinirvana-sutra. On getting the Information that the rest of the text was to be found in Kashmir Ho went to Kashmir but in vain. Ho then went over to China Ani settled in Leang-Chou where Ho translated Buddhist texts at the request of the local ruler during A.D. While translating his copy of the Mahapariniva-Nasutra Ho got the information that the complete text Could Ho found in Khotan. He then went to Khotan where He discovered a second part of the text which Ho brought back to Leang Chau and translated. The text still appeared to him to be incomplete. on getting further information that there was a last part of the text in Khotan Ho immediately started for Khotan but was murdered on the way. It is clear from the account that the original Indian text was being amplified in Khotan in the 5th century. "The Tale of Wise Man and the Fool" was a Buddhist text of Great popularity in the ser-Indian region. it is now known through Chinese, Tibetan, and Mongolian translations. fragment of a Kuchean translation is also known. although the story is similar to the Prbhasavadana of the Avadanakalpaltra it is doubtful if the text had an Indian original.

We know on the contrary that the original was collected from Khotan. an account appended to Chinese translation of 445 A.D. tells us that eight Chinese monks headed by Ho Kio went to the West in Search of Sanskrit texts. They came to Khotan and put up in the Mahavihara. The Pancavarsika-Parisad was on at that time. Teachers versed in the Tipitaka were engaged in giving daily Explanations of the holy texts. The Chinese monks attended the lectures and applied themselves to acquire knowledge of the foreign language. they took down notes in a foreign language. They took down notes of what they heard in the course of the lectures. on getting back to Turfan they reassembled their notes and made a book of it. They thought it was an Avadna and gave it a new little Kien Yu king- the sutra of the wise and the fool. A Buddhist scholar of Kucha named Li-Yen complied in the 7th century with a Sanskrit-Chinese lexicon which has been Preserved in the Chinese tripitakan. although the lexicon was Modelled after Sanskrit Kosa it contains words of Central Asian origin such as Kalama(pen), kakari(paper), Makara (monkey) Kavasi(sandal), and names of places in Central Asia and China Such as trusaka (Turk), Korttana(Khotan), Kucina(Kucha), Wu & Shu (provinces of China) Kumudana (Khumdan i.e., Chiang-Ngan capital of China.

5. ART AND ARCHITECTURE

Art and architecture also played an important role in Cultural contact between India and Central Asia. A large number of art and architectural remains were Recovered from different sites and Central Asia by great archaeologists of the world. It consists of sculptures; temples, monasteries, paintings, and Music.

SCULPTURE

 The sculptures recovered by Stein are mainly of two types:

1. wooden sculpture, and

2. stueoe stuccc.

We do not find here a stone sculpture because the stone was not in practice when Indian Buddhist art traveled in different parts of Central Asia. It is a well-known fact that the Gandhara art of Northern India had its influence on the art of Central Asia which flourished from the 1st to 4th century A.D.1 We will therefore discuss Gandhara elements in the Buddha figure in the following pages. The Buddha images from Tumshuq and Kizil delineated in different positions with various gestures are carved after the poses popular with Gandhara art e.g. standing Buddhas with Abhaya or Vitarkmudra and seated Buddha in Dhyanasena.2 Another striking feature regarding the standing Position of the Buddha borrowed from Gandhara By the sculpture of Tumshuq and Kizil is the bent left Knee: while standing in abhya or Vitarkamudra.

3Chatarjee, c.; Art Central Asia; p. 19 (1977); New-delhi it and sutra no.1, 9, 10, 11, 14, 17.

2. Ibid: figure no.- 19,20- 25,27- 29,38- 41.

3. Ibid, figure no. 1,6,8,202,212,213,214,217,212.

The hairdress: is made after the Gandhara buddhas1. Sometimes hair is carved schematically with alternate nail-shaped Incisions2 and at times half is covered with snail-shellCurls3 KNOWN TO gandharasculpture4.

The eyebrows: are ringed and arched. there is an asloping Space between the eyebrows and the eye5 like those found with gandhara Buddha6 similar to the gandhara type we find here facial features which are generally oval inshape7. The press of the Buddha is represented in two ways.

(1) Opening mode and (11) covering mode as found in Gandhara Buddhas. The right shoulder of Buddhas is uncovered in the case of the opening mode whereas in the case of covering mode, both shoulders are wrapped in sanghati. If we examine minutely, we find that only the covering mode has been truly imitated a especially the upper hem round The neckline they are sometimes cord-like.1 sometimes twisted at the center and sometimes they are just collar-like figure no. 23 of Art of Central Asia as described by chhaya bhattacharjee is An ideal example to

1. ibid, figure no.- 23 and 42.

2. inghott I, fig. 246. Bhattacharjee, c; fig. No. 2

3. (ill. l). ibid fig. lll.

4. c.f. inghott l, fig. 272

5. c.f. no. 1,2,19,22 and 29 (Art of Central Asia)

6. c.f. inghott l figures. 268 and273

7. Art of Central Asia-1,19,22, and 29

8. Bhattacharjee; Art of Central Asia, fig. No. 1118

9. ibid fig no 1114.

illustrate what a strong influence Gandhara Exerted upon the art of Kizil. The folds of the sangha are so Similar to those found with figures in Gandhara that it is easy To assume that the sculpture has a Gandhara Buddha in front of himself.5The folds run exactly in the same direction as those found In the dress of the Gandhara Buddha, mentioned above 4 figure no. 23 shows other elements, which are very similar to the Conventional style e.g. The plainness of the Shoulders which lack folds, and muscles on the chest, Depicted through the kisanighate. The remnants of the Gandhara features can be seen in the case Of crescent and sometimes nails-shaped folds between the Legs of almost all the standing buddhas, both carved and Painted from sites located on the Northern-Silk Road. in the Case of the Buddhas from Tumshuk and Kizil these folds, Started as a rippling water pattern with the Gandhara Buddhas. Turned into rigid crescents.

The double folds used by Gandhara1 may have originated from Sassanian art. It is noteworthy that except for the oasis of Kucha, most of the Cultural pockets on the northern Silk Road show any linking for this element. The artists and sculpture of Kizil appreciated too much by Bussaghali, have commented while describing

1. c.f. no. 2 with inghott, 1, fig. 200.

2. Art of Central Asia fig no. i115. C.f. no.3 with inghott, 1,

Fig. 225.

3. ibid i116., c.f. no. 28 with inghottt, l, fig. 225.

4. is the no. of fig. of the art of Central Asia.

5. c. f. inghott. 1 fig. 233.

The style of Kumtura, a neighboring center of Kizil that on the one hand, a Chinese imprint is found in the group of sods in Tushita heaven, on the other hand, Chinese Gandhara features can be seen in the elaboration of hand, The artists and sculpture of Kizil appreciated too much with Bussaghali, has commented while describing The style of Kumtura, a neighboring center of Kizil that At the one hand, a Chinese imprint is found in the group of sods in Tushita heaven, on the other hand, Chinese Gandhara features can be seen in the elaboration of hand, In certain conventional gestures, and in the use of double out, line to emphasize specific details.

For depicting the folds of garments only, in Gandhara, a double Outline was used3, not for facial features and hand except in the scene from Tushita heaven (above mentioned). The Gandhara elements can be traced in the case of other Than Buddha i.e. The figures of Bodhi Sattavas, Gods and Goddesses, musicians, laymen, and crowns. in Gandhara art, the crown of Bodhisattvas and royal personage, generally consist of a large round medallion with tapering tension and a central jewel within the disc respectively. A semi-circular knot is found on either side of this large Disc which is elaborately carved.

1.ingbott, l, pl XXLL and fig. 125.

2. russagali, N." painting of Central Asia", Geneva, 1963.

p. 90; illustrations on p. 89.

3. Bhattacharjee. C; art of Central Asia: fig. no. 11, 13 to

18, 35, 64 and 71.

4.C. f. inghott fig. 248, 316 and 319.

5.C. f. ibid. fig. 8.

almost similar type of diagram is found at Tunshuk and Kizil. A fresco of Dadan Uliq (in the 18th century) bears testimony to the fact that Indian art Existed in Central Asia. although the pose of this feminine form evokes comparison with some examples of classical sculpture Some would compare it with the venue de medicis-the style remains Indian. any hesitation is removed when one considers the line of the arm, and stiff more that of hands, with their long flexible figures,1 the details of the jewel Etc. Moreover, the body exhibits the three inclinations, of neck, waist, and feet, showing the "Tribhanga", which brings us back directly to the Ajanta version. Wachsberger2, who has given a very minute description of this specimen, very filly Compares it with a high relief from a temple in Orrisa, a work Which has been already reproduced by haveli3. this delicate Figure and sensuous infinitely more so than that woman bathing in the Dadan-uiliq fresco, she dances before a royal personage, the right arm rounded with delicately modulated lines is slightly bent, this emphasizing in a high degree The supply, almost acrobatic impression which this dance scene offers.

1. Gupta, s. "les mains dans less fresques d' Ajanta "paris 1950.

2. Wachsberger, A;" stillikritsche stude in zur kunst chinestch

ostAsiatische zeitschrift.

3. Havell. Ideas of Indian art plate xll.

Champa and Java (Borobudur) offer similar examples deriving, it needs to be added, from the same Indian source.

ARCHITECTURAL REMAINS ON CENTRAL ASIA

In Central Asia, we find architectural remains mainly of two types (1) temples and (11) monasteries. in the early phase of their Existence at Tumshuk, Kucha, Kara Shahr, and Turfan were full of

Monastic examples. besides the monastery buildings, these places were embellished with stupas whatever remains of monasteries were available after being destroyed by Muslim invaders and treasure hunters, they amply demonstrate that These monasteries were more or less made after the Gandhara Monasteries of Indiantype. 1 We have discussed in the first chapter that the art of having temples was carried from India to Central Asia.

So, we find that the temples and monasteries were hewn from very cliffs of the great crescent-shaped mountains.2 The size of the Cave temples varied from place to place on the side of many of the temples varied from place to place. on the side of Many of the temples their study rooms and living rooms for the monk. remains of store rooms and living rooms for the monk remains of storerooms and living rooms for the monk Remains of store rooms with fixed storage containers are Still to be seen.3 this can be compared with the monastic architectural remains of Nalanda (India).

Wall paintings were used to decorate the rock sanctuaries.

If we study these wall paintings minutely, we come to conclude

1.   Bhattacharjee, c; Art of Central Asia, p. 18 (1976, India)

2.   Ibid. p. 18.

3.   Ibid. p. 18.

Our view is that these paintings were not only for decoration but also for teaching the people. In the case of temple architecture existing in Kizil, we find that They were of two types (1) This type very frequently contained a rectangular entrance hall. Buddha's figure was fixed at the back of the wall of the cella. There is a corridor on either side of this figure, a corridor at the back. It was meant for the devotes to go around for the Pradaksina or Circumbulation. The roof is generally valued the second type of temple architecture found here is on the Pattern of prison buildings, having dome-shaped roofs, the entrance hall of these domed buildings is not known since they were already destroyed. The scared scared image of worship was placed on a finely molded pedestal in from of the back wall of the cella. The roof of the cella of a cave of a painter has an interesting Roof, known as a "lantern roof". if consists of several wooden squares of different sizes arranged like a pyramid. The square Beams are placed in a way that the corners of the upper square Always lie on the middle point of the side of the square immediately Blow. it allows light and air to pass into the building and at the same time the smoke of the earth finds its way out. Similar lantern roofs were found not only in Kizil but also in Ramayan the roofs in Turfan usually have valuated Roofs. The use valuated roof is very popular throughout the Turfan Oasis, since it gives protection from excessive heat in the summer. The houses have true arches, which were made with brick being placed lengthwise along the plane of the Arch. Whatever the plan of the houses of the cave temples, The plain and the elevation of the stupa remained more or less the same as found in Gandhara. it is apparent from several Votive stupas found along the northern Silk Road1

1. w. p. from C.A. shrines.

2. p artof c a p 18.

Roofs. The use valuated roof is very popular throughout the Turfan Oasis, since it gives protection from excessive Heat in the summer. The houses have true arches, which were made with brick being placed lengthwise along the plane of the Arch. Whatever the plan of the houses of the cave temples, The plain and the elevation of the stupa remained more or less the same as found in Gandhara. it is apparent from several Votive stupas found along the northern Silk Road1.

The doorways were made after the Indian chaitya arches2. capitals of the pillars exhibit the remnants of Indian motifs, e. g. Purnakumbha3. there are also double capitals showing volutes and floral motifs4. several corbels have also come to light5. They is all either richly painted or carved. there are some Simple and beautiful painted and carved

1. fig. (1) & (11), 420, 423.

2. No. 4200 to 435

3. No. 442 -443

4. No. 444-445.

5. No. 440, 441,462,463,470,471,472,477,498,499,500.

Pedestals1 recovered from important sites on the northern Silk Road. There are several elaborately painted beams found at Turfan that bear various motifs e.g., clouds, flowers, Labyrinths, scrolls, and spirals. these beams seem to belong to a huge architectural complex.3

1.   No.   430,446,447,448,501-502,505,516.2.   No. 464,465,466,467,468,469,473,478,479,480,481,482,483.3. p. 19.

PAINTING

PAINTING OF TUNG HUANG

Mural the recovered paintings from Tung-Huang which is of Oinestimable value both for the students of Buddhism and Asiatic, Especially Chinese art. Stein has given a handful of light on these Paintings in "Ruins Desert Cathy (1912)1, Ser India (1921), And The Thousand Buddhas3.In 1918 the collection was divided, according to the agreement, Between the government of India and the British Museum. India Government has preserved it in the National Museum in New Delhi. The drawings and paintings are on Silk, linen, paper, and other Materials. three main styles are represented in the collection: -

Indian Buddhist, marked by the partial nudity of figures, and rolling Poses (head on one side, body bent at hips, one leg drawn up & C). Indian type of countenance. (11 Chinese Buddhists, marked by draping of upper body rigid, Symmetrical poses, Chinese (or at least non-Indian) type of Face. much sinicized Iranian communities of Central Asia. After all, we must believe Gray who comments:" The idea of excavating shrines from the living rock had traveled with the Buddhist faith from India. (111) Chinese secular, used in side-scenes, painting of donors

(1)   & c. this is purely Chinese, showing no other influence save, occasionally, that of Here we will discuss only the Indian Buddhist styles.

1. A. Stein - personal narrative of explorations in Central Asia and most China: Macmillan & co.; London 2 vols.

2. A. Stein - Ser Indian in 3 volumes London, 1921.

3. A. Stein -   Thousand Buddha- London 1918.

the painting of tung huang deals with Buddha and bodhisattavas, avalokitesvara Sakyamuni, lokapala, matreya, ksitigarva, amitava, dhrtarastra vajrapani manjushri, virupaka, prajapati and some female divinity. if we consider Buddha first, we find here the paintings related to the scenes from the life of Buddha, five Buddhas, with Bodhisattvas. The Indian influence on the art of paintings from Tung Huang is clear from the only examples in which Buddha is preaching under the Bodhi Tree. as described by Arthur Walay. "The Central figure is seated with legs interlocked, clad in A bright red robe. his hands are in a variety of the preaching The law mudra. his lotus seat is covered with floral scrolls. Ho Is seated on a plain green lotus pod. his canopy is upheld by two pots, the tops of which cluster the star-shaped

1. Basil Gray- BUDDHIST CAVE PAINTING AT TUN-HUANG

P. 18 London (1959).

Of which cluster the star-shaped leaves of the bodhi tree. on each side is a Bodhisattva and three bare-headed monks; on each side is the lotus seat, another Bodhisattva. none of these subsidiary Figures can be identified as the cartouches which go with Them were left blank. in the center at the bottom is the tortoise Funerary slab (Kuei pi), such as occurs in connection with Chinese tombs. it is undescribed. Of the two donors, only the woman (left) is complete. She wears a red skirt and hairdress tightly over the head into a knot of the neck. A ribbon sticks up at the top of the head. of the man's figure, only the top of the cab remains. they have been treated as the part of the painting and are not contemporary'. colours: Buddha's robe is a light vermilion. there is a prevailing tone of orange. more blue than usual, e.g., Buddha's hair. Ho Reproduced: thousand Buddhas, pl. x; kokka, 392. Painting: 4ft 6 in by 3ft. 4 in1.In an elaborate article (Kokka no. 392)2 Mr. Tanaka Kazumatsu discusses the relation of this picture to the frescoes in the Horyuji kondo and also to the Ajanta frescoes. Ho points out That the method of drawing features with shading and lights Used with realistic effects at Ajanta 3.1. ibid.

2. ibid. 3. W.P. from tung huang- p.12.

Sir Aurel Stein found highlights of this kind used at Miran and perhaps belongs to fourth century A.D.1 fig. reproduced: Thousand buddhas Pl, X Kokka 392).

SCENES FROM THE LIFE OF THE BUDDHA

Other scenes from the life of Buddha are as follows: - LXXXIV- (2) (a) upper half of the painting and inscription Last. The lower part of the figures of Suddodhana and Maha Prajapati are visible, seated on mats. two attendants Stand in front of them, and on the left, a male figure (the grand minister*), moves away as though to execute commands.

(b) King Suddhodhana and Mahaprajapati walk to the right. In front of the king walks the minister, with head turned back, as though receiving his commands. behind walk two female Attendants. (c)Buddha with a red halo, seated on a throne with the monk on his Right, addresses the king and Mahaprajapati, who are knee-lingOn mats. behind them, male attendants. on the right, the head and shoulders of the man in green the rest lost.

(d) The queen Mahaprajapati, with the grand minister on her right. The scenes are divided by the orange bands, ornamented with White Tseu-like flowers.

1. ibid, no. 12.

2. LKUIV- ibid, no. 12 as recorded by further Walley.

PAGE NO 133

On the left. on the right four bowing courtiers and three horses Men gallop down a winding path with with pennons in their hands. (b) Sakyamuni (his head alone is preserved) sits among rocks while his Kanthaka makes obeisance before him, of chandala the groom only the head is preserved. (c) return of chandaka and kathaka to the palace. The horse stands riderless before a curtain pavilion; from which two women seen are Sakyamuni, wife of Yasodhara, and his foster mother Mahaprajapati. One of them leans weeping over the horse; while the other raises her sleeve to Her eyes; Chandaka, on the left, holds up a penon. The banner retained three bottom streamers of bluish green Silk (now detached). other accessories and the upper end middle of the Painting is lost. Colours: much effaced.

Painting: l ft. Loin. by 7-1/2 in1.LXXXVLLL (3) (a) the counter with the old man on the left, battlemented City wall, with square projecting gateway and roofed Chamber above. out of this gate way sakyamuni rides on his Horse kanthaka. a courtier attends him on foot. Before him under a tree an old man leans upon a stick, attended by Another man.

1. ibid no. 118.

(b) the encounter with the sick man. The sick man sits on The ground under a tree, supported by attendants in red Coat, whilst another attendant in green offers him a drink in a bow*

LXXXIX (4) THE BIRTH OF BUDDHA:

(a) his bath in the Lumbini garden. He stands, a child naked save for red loin cloth, in an oblong basin raised on a lotus pedestal, while a stream of water falls on his head from a white and slate-colored cloud above. On either side his mother Mahamaya and his aunt Mahaprajapati with hands clasped in adoration 1. (b)The seven steps. He stands in the middle of a large Pink and white lotus, his right arm stretched up and his finger Painting to heaven; his left arm pendant.

 three other lotuses Lie round, and flowers float in the air. on the right Kneel, the two women. on the left is a man (Suddhodana) in a red coat and black cap. XCI (5) the dream of mahamaya. to the right of a Verendah lies Maya asleep on a couch. she is Wrapped in a red robe and lies on her right side. palace Buildings appear behind. in the center above her head, on A cloud, appears a red dish, in which stands an elephant with an infant Buddha on its back.

Ibid. p. 120.

1.   Ibid. p. 120. (Very roughly indicated) in the left bottom corner stands a woman attendant holding a fan. (b) birth of Sakyamuni. on the left, a weeping willow with red Stem. under it kneels a woman attendant holding up white cloth for the reception of the infant. in the center stands Mahamaya, her right Hand raised grasping a bough of the tree, an attendant behind Holds her left

hand. The infant springs its head downwards under the right arm. on the right edge two women and in the Background large pink lotuses with slate-coloured leaves Growing on thick red stalks. Paintings   1 ft. 3 in by 7-1/4 in 1. C V BODH SATTAVA (perhaps manjushri)-fragment figure (lost below the knee was standing facing the spectator. Right arm bent up at elbow hand extended palm upper Most, holding between finger and thumb long stem of pink Lotus on which rests a book. left hand raised before the breast, Palam out, thumb third finger joined.2 skirts of transparent White stuff, spotted with red, over green langoti, stoles of dull red, green, and brown. small curls along the forehead. Remains of yellow paint on the right hand. Painting oft. ll in by oft. 7-1/2 in.

1   Ibid. 122.

2   Ibid. 131.

LXVI AVALOKITESVARA (INDIAN TYPE) is an oblong Central panel framed by a border of Vajras containing a large Avalokitesvaras seated in Lalita Pose. left knee is raised, and their left hand hanging over it holds a rosary. circular vesica, narrow horseshoe halo, Black ringlets on the shoulder, pear-hung jewelry, and canopy. Details of head and features affected. in corners above, two Small seated Bodhisattvas, and below, a Bodhisattva and Conventional lion seated on either side of the vase with flowers, affected by over painting of foliage and birds. round the edge Are placed alternately, on lotuses, eight emblems of Avalokitesvara of the emblem, the wheel of the law, and the vase are at the top. on the left is a vajra bell and on the right is a fish. The two lower emblems are defaced. The wheel, vase, and bell occur as emblems in the paintings of the thousand-armed Avalokitesvara. Avalokitesvara with the Fish (or with the fish basket) is one of the thirty-three Forms of Bodhisattva.

Colors most effaced built applied over a coat of white, as in CXL, NO. border Painting: 4ft. 0 in. by 2ft. 9 in.

(1)   (a) Avalokitesvara stands facing the spectator. right hand raised to shoulder and turned backward, thumb and first finger joined; left hand in Vitarka mudra at the breast. Retains head pieces border and remains of a streamer of light Buff linen. Colours: much faded. Dhyani Buddha (Amitabh) in the headpiece.1

(b) Avalokitesvara stands facing spectators with hands in Anjali mudra. ragged and incomplete at the edges and bottom, but Retains the headpiece. Painting- 3 ft. 9 in. by oft. 9 1/2 in.2 CCXCL.

(c) cc. 0022 Avalokitesvara stands facing the spectator on two small lotuses. right hand raised supporting willow Spray on palm; left hand by side holding a flask. dhyani Buddha on tiara. figures and dress of Indian type. border lost. Colours: almost gone from flesh, halo, and lotus-stand. Otherwise limited to rather dirty red, brown, and green.

Painting: l ft. 6 in b-y lft. 0 in.3

CDXCLLL SAKYAMUNI (A. D. 949) (ch. XiVi 008).

Sakyamuni sits crossed-legged on a lotus seat upon a railed Terrace rasing from the lake, attended by Shakas bodhisattavas and four aimed lokpalas. At top of

1   Ibid. p. 155.

2   Ibid. p. 155

3   Ibid. p. 217(painting in the museum of Central Asian antiquisites, delhi). CCXCI- the numbers in brackets are those of Sir Stein's list in INDIA pp 937-1088.

Picture, ten small Buddhas, with inscribed cartouches (the

Length lost). Sakyamuni has a right hand in Vitarkamudra; and a left-hand pendant with the thumb touching the third figure. Below are donors: a man carrying a smoking censer kneels, attended by a boy carrying a fan on ple. He wears a straight straight-brimmed hat.

On the other side a lady with elaborate coiffure (may combs and pins) attended by a girl. Inscriptions: only one of the Buddha's names is fully legible 'Prise of the Buddha of the merit of precious signs, The Third name begins with visvabhu.

the next ends in muni These are probably ten buddhas of the past, predecessors of Sakyamuni. The names, in so far they are legible, do not Accord with the usual enumerations of the buddhas of the ten Quarters, and for that reason it seems better to identify the Central figure as Sakyamuni and the ten minor buddhas as his predecessors, rather than to accept the painting as simplified "Paradise of Amitabh" the Central inscriptions is almost entirely Effaced, but the date second-year seventh month (A. D. 949) Is legible.1 The picture is complete with an inch border and suspension Loops of purple Silk.

---

1. ibid p. 285.

2. the seventh month began this year on the 28th of June.

Painting: almost intact but surface worm and colouring effaced.

Colours: mush effaced robe of Buddha and platform red.

Considerable use of dirty blue. CCXV AMITABHA AND ATTENDENTS, with side scenes showing the Cch 0051 legend c. Amitabha has right hand in vitarka-mudra. left-hand palm Upward on lap. The two chief Bodhisattvas sit with one Leg pendant and one bent. between each of them and Buddha sits headed descriple. The robes and ornaments of all the Bodhisattvas are of 'Indian' type, with narrow scarves only Across the breast and narrow stoles leaving most of the body and Arm bare. The musicians on the platform below play (from Night to left.) need-organ (sheng), flute, clappers, and pipe the dancer hold a scarf. of the buddhas in the bottom corners Only the head and shoulder remain, and of the lake only a small Part.

Side scenes: On the right legend of Ajatsatru.

(1) Buddha appears to Vaidehi as she is walking.

(2) Vaidehi throws herself down before Buddha who again Appears on the lotus seat.

(1)   Ajatsatru pursues his mother with a sword. Minister Candraprabha and the doctors are ready to intervene.

(1) Vaidehi visited Bimbisara in prison, giving him a drink Concealed in a lotus garland.

(1) Ajatsatru on horseback meeting the garter of the prison, who bows obsequiously. Behind, a lector with club.

(1) Destroyed: parts of the pavilion with Vaiddehi (7) seated inside. On the left, is the meditation of queen Vaidehi.1

Colors: The flesh has been pink-white, but the paint has chipped away. the general tone of red-brown paintings in by 3 ft., 8 in. CCCLL (ch. 00163) Maitreya Bodhisattva (linen banner) Standings figure, three-quarters right. hands in anjali Mudra. much effaced. inscribed Maitreya Bodhisattva.

Paintings 2ft. 5 ½ in by 0 ft. 6 1/1 in. CCLVI (ch. 00163) MANJUSRI

CCLVI (ch. 00163) MANJUSRI (paintings on paper) Sits on the back of the white lion, with a left leg pendant. Right hand raised in species of Vitarka-mudra. the left-hand holds wishing Staff across the breast. back attendant holds the lion by a ribbon attached to the collar. on the left, a woman in a tenth-century headdress.

1. Ibid. P. 218.

2. Ibid. P. 221.

Before her kneels a naked boy, holding up a lotus bud between His palms. Inscriptions:

(a) on left: Manju Sri pu-hsien Sattavabodhi, first among expositions. The female convert offers...., This translation is very tentative, as the inscription is by an illiterate person who uses the wrong characters in the wrong orders.

(b) On right: eight daughters of the family .... Teachers, Masters, heart one (meaning not clear). Colors: 'black' attendants and cloud, on which the lion Stands are dark macive. lion's mane, green, robes, orange and green. Reproduced-SER INDIA PL. XCI1

Painting: lft. 7 in. by 0 ft. ll in. CCCLXLL (ch. 00355).

KSHITIGARBHA AND THE TEN KINGS OF HELL Kshitigarbha sits facing spectators on a lotus seat with a metal Base. lacks the usual beggar, 's staff. which has, however, been inserted (a straight stick) on the Obverse side of the painting.

1 Ibid P. 236 SER INDIA PI. XCI.

Downside sits the ten kings, the tenth alone is armor and alone actually judging a soul.1Besides each stand two boy attendants. Below Kshitigarva, 's Knee is the kneeling priest: but the usual white lion Is lacking. donors (two men on the right and two women on the left) Are in tenth-century cost. The painting is complete Except for the border. Colors: kshitigarvas mantle is bright red, with cross bars, Left the color of the Silk under a robe, green with Flower spots in red; hood

 pink and green. Painting-2ft. 5 in by lft. 10 in2.CDVLI (ch. I. 004) Vajrapani: Stands facing spectator, feet apart, head three quarters left, Hands carrying long vajra with fleming jewel at top. Top pieces and side streamers lost; but bottom streamers and Weig ting bpoard well preserved. Colors include coil (above blue halo), and the usual mauve purple. Stole, cloud blue and green on the reverse. Flesh, grey tinted

With pink. Reproduced-thousand Buddha PI. XXIX.Painting-2ft.

1 in by oft. 67/8 in.1. Ibid. p. 240.

2.   ibid. p. 240.CDLV (Ch. XXIIOO33) Prajapati (painting on paper): The divinity rides on a peacock, holding a flaming jewel in the right hand and a cock in the left. Colours: Indian red and greyish green and blue.

CJX DHRTARASTRA* GUARDIAN OF THE EAST:

Upper and of painting lost and all accessories, except three Out of four bottom streamers of light brown Silk. He stands three-quarters left on the back and hand on the demon, who rests on his knees and elbows, Ho holds an arrow at his breast with winged in his left hand. in his left hand, the demon grasps A red scaly snake with gaping, dragon jaws1. dharmasastra has no mantle on the tiara but wears instead a helmet with a wide curling Rim and orange plums. sausage-shaped collar clasped under the Chin. No. scale armor is shown, but we may suppose that it is Covered by the white doublet that Ho wears. but the greenish oblong pleating at the edge of the doublet and shoulders may represent oblong scales of armor. face human, with narrow eyes, Full lips, a small mustache, and a tuft on the chin. Colors: much effaced; the general tone of yellow-green, red alone Remains strong.

1. Thousand Buddhas- Stein PL. XXIX; Ibid p. 252.

CVIII. VERURAKSHA, GUARDIAN OF THE WEST: Face spectator, standing on the head and knee of a contorted Demon. left hand at waist holds naked sword upwards and aslant Across the body, right hand supporting blade at the breast. Head turned towards the right shoulder.

the pose is that of the More Indian Lokapalas. scale armor round edged on shoulder Body, and skirt. skort was the red border and pleated green edge and split up in front. apron and flaps over hips are of blue Leather cut separately, ornamented with metal work and jewels. The breastplate is of light blue leather elaborately ornamented with metal work. The materials intended by the artists

Are not easy to recognize, for the picture is an intelligent Copy by a hand That tends to be more decorated. The halo is green, with a dark Carmine cloud curling above. The demon sprawls on his back, Clasping the Lokapala leg with his right hand 1.

Complete with all accessories save for weighting-broad. headpieces of cream-colored Silk with a broad edging of salmon red. suspension Loop of brocade. Side-streamers of thin myrtle-green Silk with flower and insect motifs in pastle2. Reproduced: in SER INDIA, PL. LXXXIV

Painting: 2 ft. 2 ½ in. by oft. 6 7/8 in.

Length of whole- 6ft. 1 in.

1. Ibid p. 133.

2. Reproduced in SER INDIA pi. LXXXIV. Ibid p. 132.

(B) WALL PAINTING IN ANCIENT SHRINES:

The great scholar, explorer, and traveler, Aurel Stein , Discovered a large number of wall paintings from ancient shrines in Central Asia. Fred H. Andrews, has thrown a vivid Light on these paintings.

A. K. Warder has said that the Buddha was fond of shrines1. The practice of decorating the interiors of shrines with paintings is of great antiquity, reaching back perhaps to the prehistoric Ages, when cave-dwellers drew on their wall subjects of us, unknown significance2. Ho early and hence the practice of wall painting reached India, Tibet, Central Asia, and China, on whether these lands originated their art, there Is no sufficient historical evidence Tseu no sufficient historical evidence to determine3. with the Expansion of Buddhism and the erection of increasing numbers of stupas and shrines, sculptors and painters were in constant

Demand for work on the enrichment of this sacred structure in exhaustible subject matters was provided in Buddhist legends the jatakas and when elements from richly complex Hindu Mythology were later imported into the relatively simple Cred of early Buddhism the scope for the artist was immediately extended.

1.   WARDER A. K. INDIAN BUDDHISM.

2.   W. P. FROM A. S. P. XVI

3.   IBID. XVI.

The example of wall paintings from ancient shrines is broadly divided into two parts. earliest one and latest one. The earliest are those from Miran (PI. 1 to 111) and the Latest from the interior of the Buddhist shrines M. LLL and M. V. The walls had been originally painted with subjects From Buddhist legends, but most of this had fallen.1 speculation as to the origin of the typical figures of Buddha Are many. in a fragment from Mirana, MFII, 003, plate I. There is nothing exotic about him. Ho is just an ordinary man in the act of teaching, such as many painters might draw observation from any contemporary preacher. Ho is distinguished Only by his plain nimbus and the color of his robe. The Same simple quality pertains to all the persons in the Miran Paintings. The story of the recovery of wall paintings from ancient shrines Is very interesting. in June 1900 Aurel Stein was placed on a special duty by the government in the region of Khotan. The Immediate incentive for this expedition was a communication Ho had received from Professor Buhler of the finds of birch Bark manuscripts acquired in the vicinity of Khotan, but of Which no information was forthcoming as to their exact provenance.

Stein felt that personal investigation on the spot, interrogating the alleged finders, and verifying the Exact circumstances and position of the discoveries were the

I.W.P. FROM A.S. PP. SHAKAS.

Their full archaeological value. Ho much more be achieved in This strenuous twelve-month, S tour is recorded in his preliminary Report, "Archaeological Exploration in Chinese Turkestan" And his fuller account entitled "Ancient Khotan" the route taken On This, his first Central Asian expedition, via light and Hunza into Chinese territory on the tagh-dumbash Pamir by way Of Kilik pass.

here was started his triangular and plane table Survey, which, with astronomical and geological observations, Continued throughout his journey. passing through trash kurgan, A very ancient outpost of Central Chinese dominions, and sankol, surveying by the way the mus tag at a Range with a peak of 24,000ft. There is considerable internal evidence in these paintings in favor of the probability that they are Indian in conception and execution2. The men are of Indian types, some with generous mustaches and beards; their garments are Indian; In the destroyed painting of Vessantava Jataka, the elephant Shows the accuracy of form and truth of action that the Indian Artist alone can so faithfully render, the girls, although Suggestive of the Persian type of beauty, may well be Indian Perhaps influenced by contact with Persian fashion. Furthermore the inscriptions occurring in the painting are in Kharosthi, Qan Indian script used in India, and the legend of the presence

1.   Ibid. p. SHAKAS.

2.   W. P. from A. S. PXVI.

An Indian colony in Khotan in Ashoka, time helped to Strengthen the probability that Indian artists, familiar with Buddhist lore, may have found employment for their skill Along the Silk route running between Khotan and China on Which Miran stood. The partial shaving of the heads of the Garland-carrying boys is almost certainly Indian and has the Spiritual significance of ancient sanction. Now we will discuss the significance of the paintings from different shrines one by one. (4) WALL PAINTINGS IN ANCIENT SHRINES:

Now we will discuss the significance of the paintings from different shrines, one by one, painted fragments from Miran, Shrine III1

M. III.002.A male figure, perhaps that of Gautama Buddha although without a halo, is seated on a dark, rosette studded maenad, turned slightly towards the right, with his feet firmly planted on a footstool, He addresses an assembly, and his general Pose, the action of the right hand, and the emphasize Posture of the left express confident assurance in the matter of his discourse. His straight set, wide open, and Obstinate mouth indicate concentration on the argument of His audience two persons only are revealed in the fragment The figure on the right is probably a person of some consequence judging from the character of his head-dress, but assumes, with his folded hands, a bearing of reverence and rapt attention like the teacher, He is barefooted but has not foot Stool. of the other person, the drapery over the Knees and the upraised forearm only are visible. The position of the fingers, first and fourth upright and the middle two folded down seems to warm off any lurking evil influence. The headdress of the figure on the right is of a pattern that seems to be peculiar to the Miran paintings. it consists of a white, conical pagri or cap with horizontal folds or Pleats and a close-fitting head-band supporting two (or more) upstanding semi-lunar red flaps the faces are of rather a Semitic Type, with fine straight set eyes; arched eyebrows, well Separated above the nose; small but thick black mustache carefully Pointed and a thin wavy lock of hair falling in front of each ear. The hands are strong and broad with the thumb abducted and short fingernails. The food stool has 'lion' Legs, a type found also in Gandhara sculpture. The angular green patches in the foreground are rather confusing in drawing, but perhaps represent some kind of fencing On Buddhist rallies.

M III. 003.Fragment from a picture of the Buddha teaching attended by Shaka disciples. The Buddha has his right hand raised with the Thumb bent inward, touching the second joint of the third finger, that is the eight joints. This may symbolise the Buddha

Expounding the eight-fold way or the eight paramitas. The Left hand is low, probably holding up his loose robe, which is of the traditional type. his rather Semitic face is youthful, with a small but natural mustache, arched eyebrows, and straight-set open, speculative eyes. his hair rises into the Typical uses, and a thin lock hand in front of the ear. The Ears, although large are not of the grotesque length generally found in later paintings, and the lobe is pierced with a very small hole. No urans are available on the forehead the nimbus is a simple sisc. Behind the Buddha are grouped the Shaka clean shaved disciples, also Semitic in appearance, their heads arranged in two rows of three each, one above the other, the nearest to him in the upper row holding a yak-tai chauri in his raised right hand. There is a commendable attempt to impact the individual character of each of these figures. The nearest, and the eldest Has his hand appearing from inside the top of his robe, grasping Its upper edge as in some roman-sculptures-the Sophocles of theLantern museum, for instance, there is a notable delicacy in the Use of soft grey and blue rose pink in these heads. To the right of the disciples appears a naked arm with the hand Grasping a bunch of white buds or flowers, apparently In the act of throwing. forming a background of the arm is Part of a tree painted as a dark mass disappeared with red and White flowers and poppy-like leaves in greenish grey. on the Extreme left in a similar mass of black on which are scattered Well-drawn leaves in grey-blue. The flesh contour lines of the Buddha are freely drawn with a broad bush in light red, and emphasized with lines of reddish brown, along the side of the nose, line of jaw against the neck and of the forehead below the hair, around the chin, and for wrinkles in the neck, the light red only is used, giving the effect of rough shading. The eyes have brown outlined with black, black pupils, and White eyeballs, the impact of the white in some of the eyes is So thick as to catch an actual high light.

M. III .004.

These fragments which had fallen from a picture above the door of the circular cells, showing the legs of a figure standing with fact apart, turned towards the right, may have belonged to the figure whose right arm appears in M. III. 003.

The stance is appropriate to the act of throwing, in which the arm seems to be engaged. The garments, red-brown, are gathered well up the thighs and a loop of a buff stole swings out to the front, the Tseu of the right footrest on a white ground Shaded with pale grey, the flesh is bright pink shaded with warm Grey and pink. The background is back, as is also the ground color of the tree in MIII003.

M. III. 005.

Shows portions of three heads of disciples, two looking towards the left and the third downwards towards the right. The treatment is similar to that of M. III. 003, and their Same expression of individuality by variation in complexion. In the upper face is shown the grey resulting from Shaving off a heavy beard. The background is vermillion and white.

In the paintings of fragments recovered from Miran shrine we can inter that in the paintings of Miran shrines, the Bers are always drawn three-quarter fac; with large eyes Wide open but too close together, and always looking to the Side near to the front.

 the eyebrows are arched and usually well-sprinted. The neck is frequently long and always has horizontal creases. The treatment of the hair presents some interesting features. in MIII. 003, the buddhas have thick rather Curly hair, short but with a pipping lock falling in from of the ear, and a greatly amplified top-knot, which forms the usni-sa. The significance of the treatment of human hair is worldwide., and since the inexplicable indiscretion Of Samson in confiding to the perfidious Delilah the secret of his strength the hair has been subjected to many fantastic Variations, prescribed by tribal or canonical edits, the superstition of just by the equally inexorable decrees of fashion; and perhaps nowhere has this been more widely observed then In India.

PAINTED PRAAMENTS FROM TARHAD BEGYLLAKT: SHR INC XII: F. X II 007, 008.

Two seated Buddha figures from a diaper of such figures at the south corner of the shrine. The upper figure (008) is Seated on a blue padmasana in an attitude of contemplation, the head slightly titled looking towards the left. The hands on the left lie on the right and the tips of the thumbs touch in from of the body. The close-cropped black hair Has a well-developed top knot (Unisa). The ears have greatly Elongated lobes pierced with long slits.

the flesh in Grejish Tones is delicately shaped and there is a grey shaded and there is a blue grey line along the lower part of the white of the eye the robe, which seems to cover the feet, is pale green with a red border. behind the head is a shaped pink rimbusBordered with blue and outlined with a thin white line The rasica is pink, bordered with green. The lower figure (007) differs from the other mainly in the Colour scheme. The flesh is shaded with burnt sienna and out Loned with red, but there is some confusion in the drawing of the hands. The limbus is shaded pink and the resica is green with a dark brown border. The robe is red-brown. The Padmasana Is pink the background is pale green. The parallel period of these paintings is between is between the 7th and 8th centuries A. D.

PALACED FRAGMENT FROM BALAWASTE:

Bal. 0300.

The principal subject in this fragment shows a seated three-headed divinity (Trimurti), with the head inclined slightly down Words and turned to the right. The eyes are heavy-lidded and Dreamy, with the iris and pupil a mere dot, and the outer Angle rather elongated. between the upward-sloping eyebrows, A third eye is placed vertically, and above the forehead is a White, human skull, behind which the black hair rises in a top Knot. From a part studied taenea rippling tresses fall to the shoulders. The mustache is represented by then Black lines extending well across the cheeks. grey and nude to the hips, the 'leonine' body is adorned with arcanite, armlets, and bangles, and long yellow stole twines about shoulders and Arms.

round the hip is a dark red dhoti, rising at a high point at the center. on each bare thigh, lower leg, forearm, breast, and on either side of the naval is a pair of short, black Strokes. Of the four arms, the from pair are posed very similar to those of the teacher in M. III. 003. The right holds a pomegranate against the breast and the left grasps a vajra, now perished. The Other two uphold, to right, the sun, and to left, the moon. The flesh-colored, smiling. effeminate face to the right has Elongated eyes with dots for Irish and pupil. An example of this figure, light variation is that Painted on an extremely interesting wooden panel, found by Stein at the ruined dwelling D.

VII at the ancient desert Site of Dandan Uliq in 1900. in that panel painting the Figure looks the reverse way, and instead of a pomegranate in the right hand, He holds a white object, which may be a drum (lgana) but is probably a fruit. The position of the two subsidiary hands is reversed: the smiling "(female*) head to the left and the demon to the right. The position of the sun and moon Emblems is identified provisionally wrongly in the Panel paintings as the (skra and sankha) are also transposed. In the panel, the lions are covered but the tiger skin which rises to a point is exactly as in our present figure. As the thing Below the knees is missing in our picture, the comparison Must stay here. This has been suggested that this figure, undoubtedly siva, and One of the numberless importations into Mahayana Buddhism from Buddha iconography, is adopted as one of the forms of the favorite Bodhisattava Avalokitesvara.

WALL PAINTING IN ANCIENT SHRINE

Bal. 0102.

The figure of the fragment is most probably of Bodhisattva. The patterns on the robe to the left are in Universe hands of dark red-brown, red, blue, and red, this Sequence repeating. on the red-brown band is a double row of small buff squares, and within each square is a white dot. A trailing with these squares and placed checks about them are three rows of rosettes, each formed of Four white dots arranged in a square formation. on the red hand Is a center row of long white, lozenge shape patterns, and above and below these, in the intervals, are halves of the same pattern In yellow. within each edge of the band is a wavy white line.

On the blue hand is the same arrangement of five rows of dotted Square rosette as on the red, the second and fourth rows being Buff or not and the first, third, and fifth, white. The general artifacts are harmonious and rich, and the patterns, quite Indian, are such as are commonly used in the weaving of woolen shawls at present, especially noticeable In the garments worn by figures depicted in the Ajanta cave Paintings. A small part of the replica appears on the left and seems to be bordered with pale pink and dark grey. The fragment to the right is very similar in treatment but has less of the Sos ler detail. The rose pink of one of the bands is a Natural color in this type of textile. As in most of the Pictures, the feet are clumsily drawn, with awkward, fat heels and unnatural loss. it is very seldom that the lotus leaf Is introduced in design, and its appearance here, between the Lotus flowers, shows Ho unsuitable and intractable it is The vesica has a shaded pink field surrounded by red and dark red-brown. The little white florets scattered Over the red background from another feature extensively Used in the Ajanta paintings1.

(C) WALL PAINTING IN ANCIENT SHRINE SHRINE FROM BELEZLK

Dica. XIII. 5. From the south wall of the cella. an elestical figure apsara descends on a very decorative cloud, her arms upraised and floating Draperies streaming backward as she floats siftly Down. no wings control her flight. aerial figures of human Form are rarely if ever, furnished with wings in Indian and Chinese medieval art, unless under the influence of the rapt. The only examples in the painting of this collection Are the angels and heads of Miran (plates I and IIT), and these Therefore with the Gandhara practice and so may Ho considered influenced by Western convention.

Garuda is indeed given wings; but Ho is a bird, and is often given A human body, in that incarnation presents but an inversion of the principle. Oxidization has disfigured the face of Apsara, and other parts of the picture have suffered from abrasion and flaking. The Long under robe is pale pink, the upper rove dull red trimmed with blue, and the long stoles and sashes pale pink and blue.

the first leats of the sleeves on the forearms are similar to those of jakies on plate SHAKAS and SHAKAS. Below the apsara the rolling clouds are designed with true Chinese fancy, in which the vapor masses are gathered into floral forms, in color reflecting that of the draperies; and adapted as a repeating Ban of ornament, now very fragmentary, between the two discolored Bands above. these two bands seem to have been Varnished to make the surface sufficiently hard to bear the Pressure of some kind of broad-tipped qalam with which the Inscription in very formal Brahmi characters has been written. The background of the apsara is dull pinkish red.

RAISED FRAGMENT FROM KARA KHOJA:

The fragments were recovered from ruined shrines within the Ancient town of Idikut Shahri, about one and a half miles from rare khoja in the Turfan basin. Kao II. 02.

It was in an extremely bad state shattered and aboard, but in many ways attractive. reassembling and mounting it was A work of some difficulty and patience, and although the general Scheme is clear the details and coloring need elucidation. The scheme of the design is intended to show a region of Counters, where nine trees flourish and forest fauna make their home. The mountains are represented by a series of imbricated Lozenge shapes, with serrated upper edges, variously Coloured, with pleasing effect. The lower Central lozenge is pale green with serrations boldly outlined in dull red. that to the right is white with dull red edges. to the left, dark Red with darker red edges. The upper Central lozenge is the Samo as the lower one. The colors repeat vertically red over red, white over white, and green. this results in a regular sequence of changes of colors horizontally and obliquely. in each lobe of the serrations is a small dark spot Which was originally, a patch of gold leaf.

Each lozenge forms the background to a group of three figures: an enthroned bodhisattva, or the Buddha, with an Adoring figure kneeling at each side, two very incomplete Divinities are visible, one on each of the green lozenges. The upper one, whose head, neck, and right arm only Remain. look onwards towards a kneeling figure on his right, to whom Ho seems to extend his right band. To the Buddha's left, A second figure sits in an attitude of devotion, gazing up at him the flesh of the Buddha is pale, slightly shaded with grey. The hair is mauve-grey against a red nimbus, surrounded by grey-green. The vesica is green with red and mauvegeey Borders and above it is Borders and above it is visible the top of stylized bodhi tree in black and white. The devotee on the buddhas right, large portions of whom are Missing seems to wear a simple mauve grey tunic bordered with Buff, reaching to the knees, and Ho kneels on a green mat. To the left, in the red lozenge, appears the side of a throne, similar to that already described, but with latticed panels of mauve, red, and green.

6. CONCLUSION

After reviewing the archaeological as well as literary Sources of Chinese, Central Asian, and Indian origin we decided that there was a good relationship Between India and Central Asia from the earliest time to the 10th century A.D. as the people of Central Asia were less cultured in comparison to Indian, they adopted the customs and manner along with the other elements of Indian culture. they came in contact with human nature to explore the unknown world around them, trades, and commerce along with the missionary zeal of Buddhists and Hindus. It is a universal truth that whenever an Inferior culture comes in contact with a superior one, it grasps the elements of superior culture. The same was the case with Central Asian people.

Even the tribes that attacked Indian territories from Central Asia and ruled over some parts of it gradually vanished from Indian society. we have references to Shakas, KuShanas, Huns, and other tribes of Central Asia in this connection, who lost their separate existence After the great ruler Harsavardhana. The Indian authors established their principal colonies on the southern-Silk route have been identified as Kasagar (Saildesa), Yarkand (Chokkuka), Khotan(Khotamna), Niya, Dandan-oil, Endere, Lou-lan, and Miran, while those on the Northern-Silk route were Located at Aqsu (Bharuka), Kucha (Kuchi), Karashar(Agnidesa) and Turfan etc.

Even the kings of Central Asia bore the name of Indian origin i.e. Khotan kings wrote their name By prefixing "VIJITA" i.e VIJITA SAMBHAVA, He was the first king to introduce Buddhism in Khotan and was followed by 13kings ending with VIJATAK KIRTI, Who was a powerful king reputed to have carried arms into India in the 3rd century A. D. when Huen-Tsang visited Khotan, during his return journey VIJITAdynasty was ruling (according to Chinese and Tibetan Annals).in the case of Kucha too HARIPUSA, SUVARNAPUSA, HARADEVA, SUVARNADEVA, etc. are the name of kings, no doubt of Indian origin. We find Indian religions in Central Asia-Buddhism and Hinduism in the case of Hindu religion we find Ganesa, kumara, the sun and the Moon in the Tung-Huang, and a few other paintings of Central Asia. From endure a wooden panel was recovered with an impression of Ganesa. They were also acquainted with sacrifices i.e., horse sacrifice (Ashvamedha); Indra (Gods of Gods), and other female deities of India.BUDDHISM was the most popular religion in Central Asia Both forms- HINAYANA AND MAHAYANA of Buddhism were in practice. Miran paintings and the great cave of the "Thousand Buddha" are burning examples of Buddhism In Central Asia. Huen Tsang & Fa Hien speak of several Buddhist monasteries scattered throughout Central Asia with monks and nuns, following the Rules of VINAYA PITAKA.

Several Buddhist philosophers visited Central Asia for its propagation. some Central Asian monks also came to India to seek true knowledge of Buddhist Texts. Indian language and literature also played an important role in the literacy field. Sanskrit, Pali, and Prakrit were popular among the Central Asian people. They were also acquainted with Indian drama and medicinal texts. Last but not least, the impact of the art and architecture of India on Central Asia was visible. The paintings from Tung-Huang and wall paintings from different Shrines of this region also show the Indian influence. The sculpture and paintings recovered by Stein in the ruins of the oases of Khotan and Kara Shahr near Turfan reveal a mixture of classical and Indian styles.

Relieves decorative carving in wood from ruined restores shrines site and KHORA.

1. relieveo panel, just showing a small seated Buddha.

2. miniature (Lac corinthian capital.

3. miniature Stein Graeco-prudish style with relief scenes from Buddhist legend.

4. statue Ho in Chinese style representing a lokapala.

5. relievo of seated Buddha. KHORA. & lpRt. Sita le style cast.

7."Bibliography"

Andrews, F. H.-   wall-paintings from ancient shrines in Central AsiaLondon 1948.

Bagchi, P. C.-   - India and Central

Asia, Calcutta 1955. —

India and China. - - -

Le canon bouddhique on chine. 2 vols.

Banerjee, P.-   - Indra from Balawaste (Central Asia), indo-Asian culture. Oct. 1968 vol. 1968 vol XVII NO. 4.

- Hariti-Lakshmi from Dandan uliq in Central Asia, Paper read at

an international conference on Central Asia. New Delhi 1968.

Beals, s.-   Buddhist Records of the Western World; vol London 1906 pl. XXX.

Bhattacharjee, c.- Art of Central Asia; Delhi 1977.

Banbury   - History of Asian Geography.

Bussagali, M. -   - painting of Central Asia, Geneva 1963. - Indian influence in Central Asia, 5000 years of the art of India. Bombay 1972.

Chakravarti, N. P.- - India and Central Asia. - L' udanvarga Sanskrit.

Dabvids. R.   "Buddhism." London. 1877

 fa hsien   -   the travels of fa-hsien 399-414 A.D. OR record of Buddhist kingdoms, translated by H. A. Giles, Delhi 1972.

Gafurrow, B.- The Great Civilisation of the Kushans; COURIER (UNESCO), Feb-1969 pp. 4-12.

Foucher, Av-   L' art Greco- bouddhique du gandhar.

Gokhale, B. G.   Ancient India, Calcutta 1962.

Gray, B.   -   Buddhist cave paintings at Tun Huang; London 1959.

Gupta S. P. -   - foreign influence in the Buddhist- paintings From Khotan, Central Asia; the researcher

              (B. R. A. M.) vols. VII IX

              1966-68, pp. 41-46.

Gupta, S. P.-   - - some aspects of Buddhist art in Central Asia, SANSKRIT; A.N. Jha felicitation.

              Volume. New Delhi 1969 pp. 43 ff.

Halide, M.-   Indo-Iranian Art, "Encyclopedia of World Art" vol. –VIII. London 1963pp. 15 See also Rowland op. cit. pp. 251.

Hambis, "Asia, Central". encyclopedia of World Art pp. 827.

Ingholot, H. - Gandhara art in Pakistan, New York 1957. Pl. 376.

Kumagai, N. - "The Art of Chinese Turkestan; monumental Ser India, vol. V KYOTO 1962 pp. 90

              Figs. 165- 66.

Le coq, A. von- -buried treasure of Chinese Turkestan An account of the activities and adventures of the second and third German - Turfan expedition; London 1928-   -   Di buddhistiche spike in Mittel

Asien, orster teil; Berlin 1922.

Majumdar P C   HINDU COLONIES IN FAR EAST", Calcutta 1963.

Marco Polo   -   The Travels of Marco Polo; the Yule Edition, Airmont publishing company;

Inc., NEW YORK 1969.

Matsumoto Euchi   - tongko-ga no kekyu; TOKYO 1937 vol- 1 Pp. 732-33 and 735.

Pelliot, P.   – "Indian influences in the early Chinese Art in Tun-Huang," I. A. L. 1926.

Pelliot, P.   - -   le grottes de   Touen-houng; PARIS 1921.

Rice, Tamara Talbot -Ancient arts of   Central Asia. London 1965.

Rowland, B.   - The art and architecture of India, penguin books; Great Britain; 196 - - "Art along the Silk Roads; a reappraisal of Central Asian Art".

H J A S, Vol. 25, 1964-65

Pp. 248- 64.

Sivaramamurti, C. – "A brief survey of Buddhist art In other Asian countries"

Shastri, S. H.   - MC Crincle's Ancient India as Described by Ptolemy; ed. S. M. Shastri, Calcutta, 1927. 12 ff.

Stein , M. A.   – sand-buried ruins of Khotan; London: 1904. - - Ancient Khotan; 2 vols. Oxford 1907. - - - Ruins of deserted Cathay, 2 vols. London 1912.

- - -   Thousand Buddha; London: 1918.

- - - -   Ser India; 5 vols. Oxford: 1921.

- - - - -   Innermost Asia; 3 vols. Oxford 1929.

- - - - - -   On ancient Central Asian   tracks;

Stein , M. A. - - - - - - -   London: 1933.

Tseu, G.   - "Preliminary report on an Archaeological survey in swat" East and West; vol. IX. 1958, pp.279-328; and several other papers in the volume of East and West.

Watters, T.   -on yuan chwang; Travels in India Volume: 2; pp. 271 r, 294. Warder, A. K. - Indian Buddhism

Seated BUDDHA.

5th cent A. D. TUNSHUQ

(A) Standing BUDDHA, 6th cent A.D.; KIZIL: last Temple, last closure

(b) In the 6th century AD Tumshuq: a small ruin in the northwest of

Pelliot ruin (standing Buddha).

(C) standing Buddha, 6th cent A.D. Kizil: temple above the casket cave.

Figure.

Felico   t   &   c   i

Terracotta and

Miniature shields

In stucco from

Ruined shrines,

MING-of site,

KARA SHAHR.

Miscellaneous wood

Carving and stucco

Relieves from sites of

Ming-ol', KHORA,

Thousand BUDDHAS.

TUN HUANG LIMES.

Chuckals and busts from relicvo decoration of Dained Buddhism shrines, 'MING OL' site, KARA-SHAHR Helmeted heard, 2. 3. Heads 2 3 heads in naturalist style 467 Female busts 5. divine male bust.

M. AUREL STEIN